To Veronica and Harry £5

When they decided to move to

Norfolk at Christmas

With love from Anne.

NORFOLK

BERNARD E. DORMAN

NORFOLK

B. T. Batsford Ltd
London

First published 1972

© Bernard E. Dorman 1972

Text printed in Great Britain by Northumberland Press Ltd,
Gateshead, Co. Durham. Plates printed and books bound by
Richard Clay (The Chaucer Press) Ltd, Bungay, Suffolk for
the publishers B. T. Batsford Ltd, 4 Fitzhardinge Street,
London W.1

ISBN 0 7134 0073 0

CONTENTS

LIST OF ILLUSTRATIONS

ACKNOWLEDGMENTS

The Author and Publisher would like to thank the following for permission to use photographs in this book: Dorothy Ashley, 6; Hallam Ashley, 7, 8, 10, 14, 19, 21, 24; Barnarby's Picture Library and R. F. B. Mills 9, 18; J. Allan Cash 20, 29, 30; Noel Habgood 5; A. F. Kersting *frontispiece*, 3, 12, 16, 17, 23, 26; Pix Photos and G. F. Allen 13, 22, 25, 27; Kenneth Scowen 2, 15, 28.

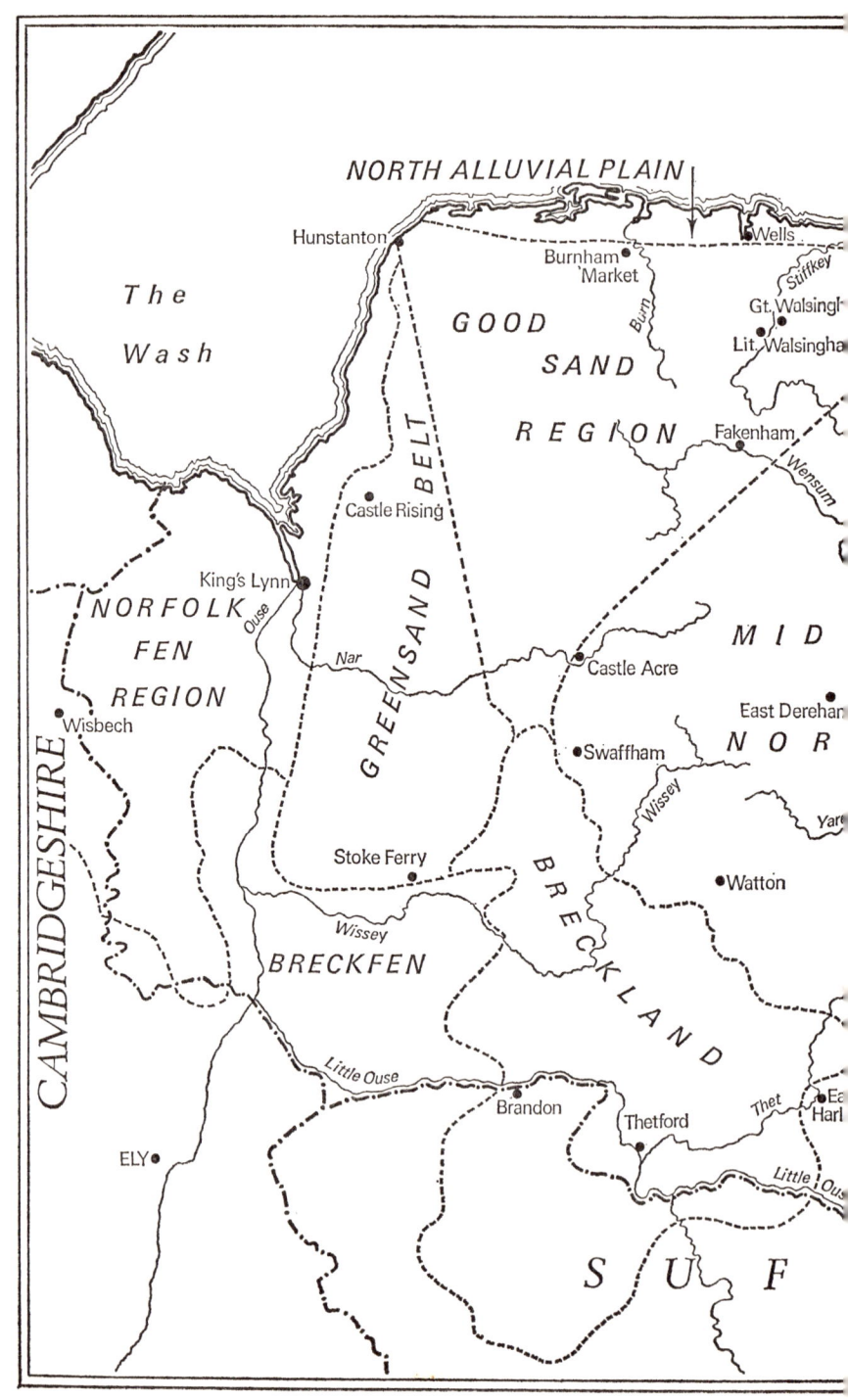

NORTH ALLUVIAL PLAIN

Hunstanton

Burnham
Market

Wells

Gt. Walsingh
Lit. Walsingha

Suffkey

The

Wash

GOOD

SAND

REGION

Fakenham

Wensum

Castle Rising

King's Lynn

NORFOLK

FEN

REGION

Wisbech

Ouse

Nar

GREENSAND BELT

Castle Acre

Swaffham

MID

East Derehan

NOR

Wissey

Yar

CAMBRIDGESHIRE

Stoke Ferry

Wissey

BRECKFEN

Watton

BRECKLAND

ELY

Little Ouse

Brandon

Thetford

Thet

Little Ous

Ea
Harl

SUF

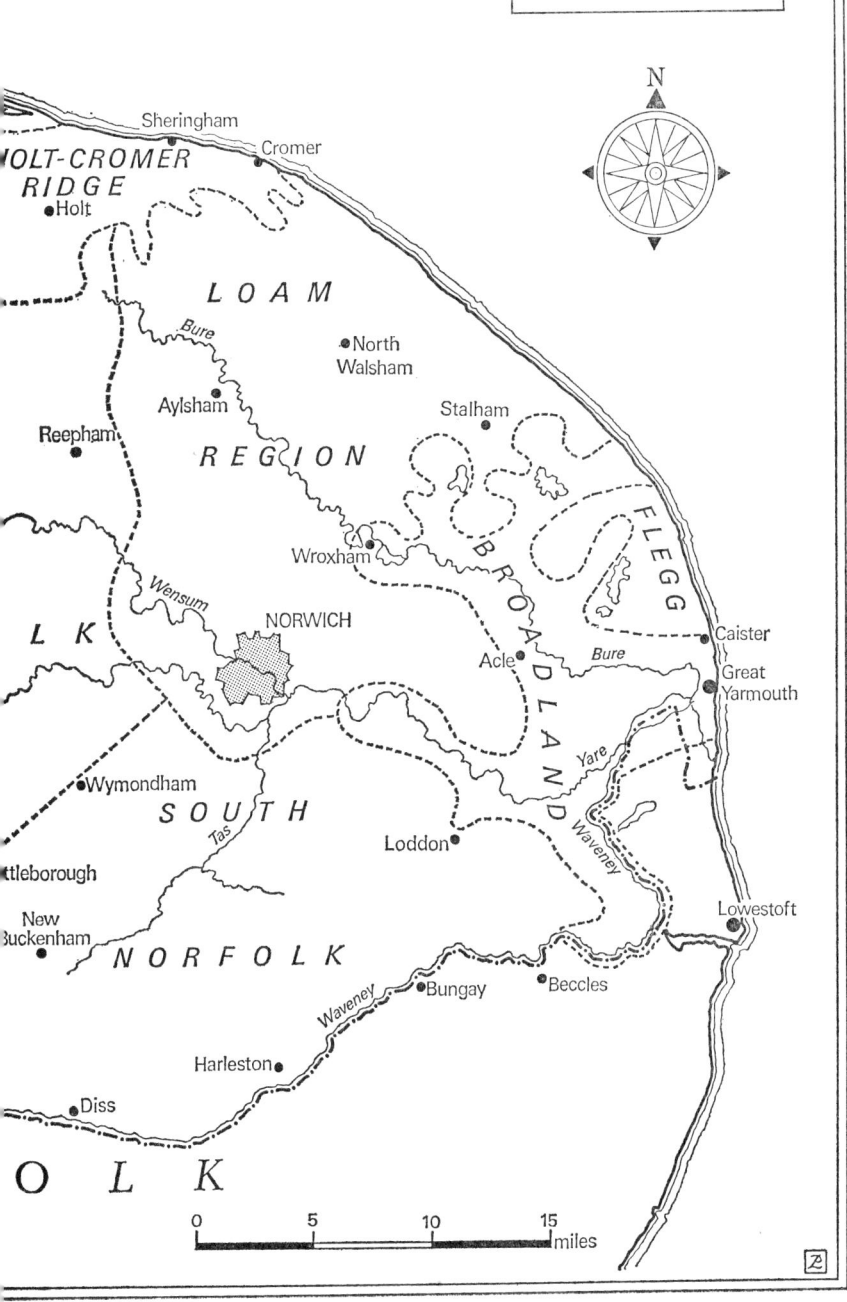

Preface

In this book I have tried to cover the main features of interest in the county without writing a detailed guide book. The tendency seems to be for an increasing number of books to be written on specialized aspects of the county by writers who have made an exhaustive study of their subject, or histories of one particular town, village or family. These books are exceedingly valuable and I acknowledge with gratitude that I have used information from a number which I have quoted in the text. It may be that the reason why there are few general descriptions of the county available, is because the task has deterred writers wiser than myself, for the result must be a book which is full of omissions: only the surface has been scratched and much that might have been described in detail has had to be given passing mention. In a book of this length, the outstanding features of the churches in the county alone would have resulted in a mere catalogue of names; the great houses, if described in detail, would have filled a book on their own; and the city of Norwich could easily comprise a volume of history and description. I have attempted to give a broad picture of the distinct regions, mentioning the features of greatest interest, and I hope that I have succeeded in conveying an impression of the scenery and character of each of them. Once the reader has been tempted to explore the county as a whole he should turn to the books dealing in detail with the subjects which appeal to him most. It is hoped that this volume will attract the reader who does not know Norfolk but would like to find out something about the county; the new resident who wishes to understand and explore his surroundings; and the visitor who needs to be guided to unusual features, either in the area he has chosen to visit or in his particular field of study. I also hope that the reader who already loves Norfolk will find some information which is fresh to him. I have sometimes remarked that in Norfolk, east is east and west is west ... for it is a big county and, as in pre-Roman times, when a belt of forest in central Norfolk separated the people of east and west Norfolk from each other, leading them outwards towards the sea in each case, now the lack of public transport on one hand, and ingrained habits on the other, produces the same result. If I can succeed in introducing the delights of west Norfolk to the inhabitants of the Norwich area and make their capital better known to the people of Marshland and King's Lynn, I shall be happy to have shared my love of all parts of the county with others. Natural curiosity and the opportunity provided by my work have enabled me to explore every part of the county over a quarter of a century, watching the changing scene through the seasons and seeing it in all weathers, seeing it too as it really is while its people are at work and not at weekends when traffic and daily life are not normal. The person who opts for a day off on Saturday when it might be possible to choose a day earlier in the week, misses a great deal; he also makes a rod for his own back and for the backs of others by increasing congestion on the roads and in the places he visits.

Norfolk, as we shall see later, is very rich in curiosities of every kind. Its hundreds of ancient churches provide a rich field of study for anyone interested in history, brasses, stained glass, etc., and many of them are outstanding. The great houses, Oxborough, East Barsham, Blickling, Felbrigg, Raynham, Melton Constable, Houghton and Holkham, enable one to follow the development of architecture and ways of living, in an unbroken sequence through three centuries. At one time there were 59 monastic houses in the county and the remains of many of them can be seen, some, like Castle Acre, extensive and picturesque. The strong social conscience of the people has resulted in conservation of both natural and man-made assets on an impressive scale—a government Minister visiting Norwich remarked that the city had achieved just the right balance between preservation and development. It is a pleasant county in which to live, healthy and restful; for the same reasons it is a pleasant place for a holiday, and the numbers of people who come to the Broads, the Norfolk coast and to Norwich itself for a holiday, testifies to this.

I have already said that this is not intended to be a guide-book; there are already two excellent books of this kind: *The Travellers Guide*, published by Darton, Longman and Todd, and the *Shell Guide* by Wilhelmine Harrod and C. L. S. Linnell, both of which give the facts about each place in alphabetical order. In the Penguin 'Buildings of Britain' series by Nikolaus Pevsner, Norfolk fills two invaluable volumes. For churches only (Pevsner deals with all types of buildings), Munro Cautley's *Norfolk Churches* is the best book available. For ornithologists there is *Birds of Norfolk* by M. J. Seago, and for botanists *Norfolk Flora* by Dr C. P. Petch and E. L. Swann. On the historical side, Bloomfield's *History of Norfolk*, published in the eighteenth century, is regarded as the chief source, although incomplete. A recent reprint of White's *Directory of Norfolk* of 1845 is a more handy source of history. *Norwich—the Growth of a City* by Barbara Green and Rachel Young, published by Norwich Museums Committee, is excellent, though short, and *The Old Churches of Norwich* by Noel Spencer and Arnold Kent is to be recommended. The Broads have been described by E. A. Ellis, a local naturalist. *Breckland*, by Olive Cook, gives a good description and conveys the feeling of that area, and there is another book about the same district by J. Wentworth Day from a sportsman's point of view. The archaeology of East Anglia has been dealt with by the late R. Rainbird Clarke in a book recently reprinted, but many other excellent books dealing with all aspects of Norfolk life are unfortunately out of print. The *Paston Letters* and *The Diary of a Country Parson*, by the Reverend James Woodforde, have become classics and are always available, but the student of Norfolk life would be well advised to buy any books which interested him when the opportunity arises, for they seldom remain in print for long. I acknowledge my debt to these books and to many more, too numerous to mention.

I should like to thank Canon A. G. G. Thurlow for reading the typescript and making suggestions; my wife for help with typing and Miss Elizabeth Mills for making the final typescript and also making it possible for me to devote time to writing the book. I should also like to thank the Revd Dr John Mosby for permitting me to use the boundaries of the regions of the county from the map in his Report of the Land Utilization Survey of Britain, Part 70, Norfolk. It has not been feasible to make the chapters correspond exactly with his areas, but the chapters on Breckland and Broadland cover almost exactly the areas shown on the map, and my chapter on Central Norfolk covers the Mid- and South-Norfolk divisions. The chapter on King's Lynn and the Marshland includes both the Fen Regions and the Greensand Belt, but I have taken the coast as a whole, as a multiplicity of chapters has had to be avoided.

2 Blickling Hall: East front 1616–27

3 Houghton Hall: West front 1721–35

Introduction

Although Norfolk is the fourth largest county in England and is only 100 miles from London, it has been less known in the past than most parts of England; but it is now being rediscovered by the tourist. Brought up as I was in the West and South of England, Norfolk did not enter into my scheme of things until I settled in East Anglia for business reasons and then, while I lived at Ely in Cambridgeshire, it was only the western half of the county which I explored. Everything east of the line through Wells, Fakenham, Swaffham, Watton and Thetford, was unknown. One only goes to Norfolk if one has some reason for doing so. For geographical reasons no one passes through Norfolk on the way to anywhere else. The ports of Great Yarmouth and King's Lynn handle few, if any, passengers, and the airport at Norwich is principally concerned with local traffic.

In the past the lack of communications with the rest of England isolated Norfolk even more. In the Middle Ages and well on into the eighteenth century, when roads were bad, it was easier to travel by sea from Norfolk to the continent of Europe than to penetrate the Midlands or to visit London. The result of this isolation has been that Norfolk people have become self-reliant, self-supporting and inclined to treat strangers with caution. It is even said that this attitude to 'furriners' dates back to the invasion by the Danes, when a stranger was a potential enemy, and it is still possible to detect differences in the inhabitants of the Danish settlements (frequently bearing names ending in -by) and the descendants of the Saxons in neighbouring villages, who have failed to inter-marry. In spite of this, Norfolk has absorbed migrants from Europe to its advantage. The Flemings who

4-7 Windmills: 4 Horsey drainage mill; 5 Burnham Overy, 1814; 6 Thurne Staithe drainage mill; 7 Hunsett Mill near Wayford Bridge

came to weave the wool which was the wealth of Norfolk in the Middle Ages, and the Huguenots in the seventeenth century who introduced silk weaving and other skills, have been absorbed, though the families have retained their names sometimes in anglicized forms. There is even a colony of Italians who settled in Norwich about the time of the Garibaldi rebellion whose descendants have the features and colouring of their ancestors. However, there is a saying that it takes 20 years to be accepted in Norfolk, whether one is English or a foreigner.

If one lives in Norfolk long enough, some of the characteristics of the Norfolk people may be acquired, not by conscious copying, but by some process influenced by the pace of life or the very factors which make Norfolk people what they are. There is the mistrust of the 'furriner' already mentioned, though the passing visitor is very welcome; the tendency to ask people why they want to know, when they ask a question; the care with which one spends money earned by hard work, the surprise that outsiders don't know facts we take for granted, and so on. I have been conscious that in the course of 25 years I have picked up some of the ways myself, and I have no regrets.

One place where the Norfolk countryman will be found in a state of nature, as it were, is in the village shop—the general store which sells everything; where the proprietor is for ever washing his hands because one customer has had a gallon of paraffin and the next needs some rashers of bacon. The village post office, which occupies a corner of the front parlour in a cottage, still exists in numbers and provides a meeting place for the old age pensioners and the mothers drawing family allowances. It will probably be here that one will hear the Norfolk dialect in use. The Norfolkman does not just have an accent, he has a whole vocabulary and a form of grammar and use of words all of his own. There is an element of invention and one sometimes suspects that some highly descriptive words have been invented spontaneously by the speaker. All classes appear to take a delight in hearing exponents of the dialect 'put it on', and there have been popular and successful attempts to present it phonetically on paper. The stranger must master the idiosyncrasies of the pronunciation of place names as he will meet with blank incomprehension

8 *Cawston: fifteenth-century hammerbeam roof*

if he asks almost anyone for many places in the way they are spelled. The classic examples are *Happisburgh* which is pronounced *Haisboro'* and *Wymondham* pronounced *Windham*. One takes *Norrich* for granted until a foreigner says *Nor-which*. A fairly safe rule is that if a place name has more than two syllables the one in the middle should be omitted, as *Hunston* for *Hunstanton*. The word 'bor' as a form of address will be puzzling until it is explained as a shortened form of 'neighbour'.

Norfolk has always been, and still is, primarily an agricultural county. Wheat, barley and, since the early 1920s, sugar beet, have been the greatest arable crops. Sheep were of great importance at one time, but are now uncommon. Turkeys, ducks and chickens are all large-scale industries, and in the past flocks of geese made the journey to London on foot when it came to the time for them to go to market. Pheasants are so common that they are sometimes referred to as 'Norfolk sparrows'. In the past the harvest from the sea has been another source of Norfolk's wealth, though this has declined for reasons which are not very clear. At one time the herring fishery brought vast quantities of fish to Great Yarmouth and made Yarmouth bloaters famous. Along the coast, shellfish and Cromer crabs have contributed to the menu. Norfolk is one of the cider-producing counties, with works at Attleborough. Market gardening flourishes in certain areas and the horticultural produce of the Marshland is dealt with elsewhere in this book.

Norfolk is a county of market towns. Norwich, a provincial capital if ever there was one, has been a market town for a thousand years and until about 1960 agriculture took precedence on Saturdays, when the great cattle market, the largest in England, was held under the shadow of the Castle. Herds of cattle were driven through the streets and motor traffic resented being put in its place of lower priority. By moving the market to a fine modern site on the outskirts, Norwich has lost a great deal in character and, incidentally in business, for Saturday is no longer the busiest day of the week in many of the shops which catered for the farmer and his wife who came to market. The tradition of market day is still strong in the only two other large towns in Norfolk, Great Yarmouth and King's Lynn. At Lynn, as it is called locally, there are two market places, one for

9 *Wymondham: the market cross, 1617*

Tuesday and the other for Saturday. The poultry market at Diss is important and the other market towns, East Dereham, Fakenham, Aylsham, North Walsham, Watton, Thetford, Swaffham, Downham Market, Wymondham and Harleston, and some smaller ones, all present busy scenes on their particular day, with stalls in the market place or main street and a sale yard with auctions of pigs, poultry and miscellaneous property. They provide an opportunity for people, often living in isolated places, to do their shopping and other business and to meet their friends. The almost universal ownership of cars, and Norfolk has the highest ratio of cars to inhabitants of any county in England, has made it possible for people to get to their market town more frequently than in the past and business has benefited by being spread more evenly over the week than it was when the village bus, which in many cases, ran only once a week, was the main means of transport.

The market towns provide entertainment. Most have a cinema and there are thriving dramatic and operatic societies in many. An apparently sleepy town can have a good deal of social life beneath the surface. There is also a tendency for church life in the market towns to flourish, sometimes at the expense of surrounding villages, and the churches at Wymondham, Fakenham and North Walsham, for example, attract large congregations and have the facilities such as large, well-trained choirs, which small village churches cannot emulate. The Norfolk market town provides the legal, medical and cultural services for the district. Most have excellent libraries provided by Norfolk County Library, the largest organization of its kind in England. Yet with all these activities only East Dereham has a population exceeding 8,000, and the average size of a market town is round about 3,000 inhabitants. But how much better to live in a place like this than in a large town! There is the fact of knowing and being known; the fact that people are interested in each other. The possibility of being able to help in the government of the place and in the running of the various activities, rather than being a passive receiver of entertainment provided by others, that makes life so much richer for people in comparatively small communities. There is a continuity, the settled population which lives in the same place generation after generation, and it is not only the native who remains in his own town. The people who come to Norfolk for business reasons, or the wife or husband who come to live in the county through marriage settle down as well. No greater compliment could be expressed. A newcomer to Norfolk who had the opportunity to make a peregrination of the county and to meet many people in a short time, remarked that the thing which struck him most was this sense of continuity. I have already mentioned the evidence of Saxon and Danish settlement, but he told a tale of two parishes which did not seem to mix with each other and he was told that it was because they had been on opposite sides. 'Opposite sides of what?' he asked. 'They were on opposite sides during the Civil War' was the answer.

Many old families in Norfolk have lived in the same place for centuries and they are not only the landowners such as the Cokes, and Townshends, but the farm workers as well. Old-established businesses in Norwich and elsewhere have been carried on by the same families for 200 years or more. Like the farmers they have thrived, and will continue to do so, by quality—doing their job well. Norfolk is not so subject to booms and slumps as other parts of the country. Its stability is an example to an unstable world.

The people of Norfolk are the product of their environment and the environment is governed by geological and geographical conditions, which in turn affect the climate. The person from outside who thinks about Norfolk at all may dismiss it as 'Norfolk Broads and all that. Very flat'. The country in fact undulates and in places rises to 300 feet above sea level. There is a steady rise in the land from east to west, with a sudden fall to the Fens. There are wide river valleys, sometimes with steep sides, and Norwich itself is very hilly. Even the country between the Broadland rivers is by no means entirely flat. Flatness is a matter of degree and compared with the Lake District, Derbyshire and similar districts Norfolk could rightly be regarded as flat, but when compared with its immediate neighbours, Lincolnshire and the Isle of Ely, it is hilly.

The underlying stratum of Norfolk consists of a deep bed of chalk which is tilted downwards towards the North Sea. The western edge of the chalk rises to about 200 feet above sea level and drops sharply towards the river Great Ouse and the Fens beyond. The chalk is mostly over-laid by other formations, along its western edge by carstone, the only *workable* building stone to be found in the county. It is a form of greensand and is brown in colour. The Breckland, which comes next, has a layer of drifting sand which at one time made this large area into a veritable desert, but afforestation has stabilized the soil and changed the character of the scenery. In the northern and central parts of the county there are the remains of glacial morrains in the forms of steep hills, and there is much gravel in the river valleys. The sands which have proved a menace in Breckland take a different form farther north where they are known as the 'Good Sands', and it is in this area, particularly round Holkham, that the great developments in agriculture took place in the eighteenth century. Flints are scattered over the surface of the fields and, with the carstone of west Norfolk, they constitute the only building stone in the county. The central and southern parts of the county consist of rather heavy clay: a forest in prehistoric times, which was cleared by Romans and Saxons, and there are wide river valleys with streams which must have once been a great deal larger than they are at present. South Central Norfolk is a highly cultivated arable region and is perhaps the least interesting part of the county, except for its churches and the old buildings in places such as New Buckenham. It is an area of clay-lump cottages and moated farmhouses, and one is seldom out of sight of one of them. Towards Great Yarmouth the geological deposits are more recent; in fact the sandbank upon which Yarmouth is built had grown out of the sea in historic times. The shape of the coastline here has changed completely since the Romans settled at Caister and Burgh Castle. The Broads themselves owe their origin to the deposits of peat which were removed for fuel in the course of centuries. The Marshland in the western part of the county beyond the Great Ouse, though administratively part of Norfolk, has nothing in common with the rest of the county. It is one with the fens of the Isle of Ely and Lincolnshire and is absolutely flat, the southern part composed of peat and the northern part, which is the true Marshland, of silt. Both parts are reclaimed land and have been the scene of constant efforts to drain away flood-water for the past 2,000 years. Huge fields of sugar beet, potatoes and other crops are divided from each other, not by hedges but by dykes. On the silt, horticulture, rather than farming, is predominant. There are orchards and nurseries of roses and bulbs. The people look towards Wisbech, Ely and Peterborough rather than to Norwich for their needs. While lack of water is one of the problems over most of Norfolk, which has the lowest rainfall in Great Britain, in the Marshland the position is reversed and man has been preoccupied for centuries with the problem of getting rid of it.

Norfolk's geology and scenery have been influenced by the Ice Age when glaciers planed the surface of the land, removing the higher ground, and in melting, deposited the silt, clay and small stones which had been carried southwards in the ice. The melting ice scooped out the wide river valleys along which narrow streams flow today.

The geological structure of Norfolk makes for variety of scenery. Northing is spectacular, for there are no rocks or the mountains and gorges which go with them. But there is a more subtle beauty which has been and still is an inspiration to artists. The coast has no inlets, the only estuary is that at Great Yarmouth, but nevertheless there is variety. The cliffs at Hunstanton are real cliffs. Those of Cromer are lofty and imposing, though constantly being eroded. Between the two are the salt marshes beloved by bird watchers and under the protection of the National Trust. The east coast has glorious sands behind which dunes protect the low-lying country. One has the choice of seeing the sun rising or setting over the sea, and from some places doing both in the height of summer. Except in the Marshland trees are everywhere. Quite apart from the great man-made forests of Breckland, with their millions of conifers, there must be millions of trees in the rest of the county. In spite of extensive felling, many of the roads are lined with oaks which were probably planted when it was expected that in due course they would provide the Royal Navy with the 'wooden walls' needed to defend the country. There are woods, such as those on the hills behind Sheringham, copses and hedgerow trees. The Wensum valley in particular has the right balance of trees, open fields and water to make ideal countryside. In the extensively cultivated clay land in the south of the county, where the ground is comparatively flat, one can look in every direction and see so many trees that, although they are mainly along hedgerows and well spaced, at a distance they merge and close the horizon with a continuous wall. A writer in the past has described the effect as being like a forest one is always approaching but never reaches.

Norfolk scenery, more than in many other counties, is almost all man-made. With no immovable natural features, such as the high hills, large rocks, waterfalls and features found in mountainous districts, man has been able to cultivate every part of the county, or adapt the appearance of the countryside for his pleasure. The gentle contours have become still more gentle under the plough, the trees have been planted or controlled during their growth. The rivers have been tamed to flow in prescribed channels. The Broads have been found to have been created, if unintentionally, by the work of man. Until the economic pressures of two wars made the upkeep of large estates almost impossible, there were many country mansions surrounded by gardens and parkland. Some, like Sandringham, Houghton, Raynham, Blickling and Holkham, and some lesser estates, still remain; and it is noticeable that where one comes across a pretty, well-wooded tract of scenery, or finds a lake, it will nearly always be where some estate has been. The heyday for the country estate were the late-Victorian and Edwardian periods and they owed much to the fact that King Edward vii, when Prince of Wales, chose Sandringham for his country home. With its arable land and cereal crops it was ideal for pheasant and partridge shooting and many were the house parties in the season.

There are no natural, geographical obstacles in Norfolk. I have already mentioned the lack of inlets on the coast, and this results in it being possible to drive along a road which is within sight of the sea for practically the whole of the hundred-mile coastline. Except for the River Yare below Norwich, and the Great Ouse, rivers present no obstacle and there are still many fords to be found through the smaller rivers, which present no trouble except in times of heavy rain or melting snow. Norfolk had, until the Industrial Revolution, been the most intensively, and is still the most evenly populated part of England. This, combined with the large number of arable fields, probably accounts for the great network of 5,000 miles of roads which provide access to every corner, and a choice of routes at the same time. The surface of all the main roads and many of the minor roads is excellent and a quiet transformation has been taking place since 1950 in improving the roads between the market towns, straightening and widening them gradually so that it is difficult to remember what they used to be like. However, it is still possible to find narrow lanes with grass growing down the middle and trees meeting overhead. In spring, hundreds of miles of verges are covered with cow parsley, and earlier there is the whitethorn and black-thorn. Rhododendrons flourish in many places and are particularly beautiful on the Sandringham estate, though the most varied and impressive sight is at Upper Sheringham.

I was going to say that Norfolk, in the main, is not good walking country. So much cultivated land obviously cannot be walked over, and many roads have no grass verges as ploughing is done as close to the actual road surface as possible. Elsewhere hedges spring straight up from the roadside. This comment does not, however, apply in Breckland or in the part of the county between Fakenham and King's Lynn where there are wide verges, which prove useful to horsemen as well as the pedestrian. There are stretches of heathland where one can ramble in this area, and also between Holt and the sea and behind Sheringham. It is true that the Norwich District Foot-path Society has published details of walks within a 20-mile radius of Norwich but they are not apparent to the uninitiated and such footpaths as remain are not always signposted. Walking along a road with the ever-increasing traffic is neither pleasant nor safe, but there are compensations.

As I write this, I have just arrived home after walking some three miles from the outskirts of Norwich along a road which I normally traverse by car at least twice a day and the difference in the pleasure was striking. I was able to enjoy the riot of colour in cottage gardens which would remain hidden from a car, and the more sophisticated, though still colourful, suburban type of gardens of new bungalows. The difference in style between them is apparent. Then there was the pleasant well-kept farmhouse; the hedges no longer impenetrable barriers but transparent screens which allowed me to see the scenery beyond them. A village church provided a picture which I could enjoy as a composition when passing slowly, but could be taken in only in a flash, if at all, while negotiating a bend in the road by car.

Along the main road, when there was a lull in the traffic, the sound of the birds and the smell of the cows came through. When I lived in a particularly pretty part of the county some five or six miles from Norwich, I noticed with surprise how seldom one could see anyone cycling or walking for pleasure, as is the case near large towns in other parts of the country. It is cause for remark now on the very rare occasions when one sees a motorist picnicking in other than popular recognized sites. Do the inhabitants of the towns all go to the sea in preference to enjoying the countryside? Previous writers of books about Norfolk have had the advantage of exploring on a bicycle, but with the great increase of traffic this would have its disadvantages and dangers now.

The Norfolk climate has been maligned as being cold, but it is the most pleasant of all the parts of England in which I have lived. Although there is nothing between Norfolk and the North Pole, and one must confess that it never seems to get really warm at Cromer and Sheringham, there is less snow than elsewhere and the cold is not so penetrating as in Cambridge, for example. The east wind is sometimes spoken of as biting, but I find that the only wind I dread is from the north-west. Norfolk has the widest variations of temperature of any part of England. Being surrounded on three sides by the sea the winds are off-shore when the sea is warmer than the land, and on-shore when the land is the warmer of the two. Thus sea mists develop which often do not penetrate more than a mile or two inland, and on hot summer days a cool breeze springs up about four o'clock in the afternoon as the air from the sea is drawn up over the heated land and this breeze can be felt in the middle of the county. There is much sunshine and clear, wide skies.

The rivers of Norfolk are exceptional. Two of them make the county virtually an island, for the Waveney and the Little Ouse rise at the same spot where a road at South Lopham crosses a ditch; the waters of the former flow east to the sea at Great Yarmouth, while the Little Ouse flows west through Thetford and joins the Great Ouse which, in turn, flows into the Wash near King's Lynn. These rivers and the main river systems comprising the Wensum, the Yare and their tributaries, which flow eastward to the sea at Great Yarmouth and include all the rivers of the Broads—the Bure, the Ant and the

Chet—are slow-moving streams whose waters seem to be stationary, reflecting their banks and the passing clouds and conveying a sense of peace. But the rivers which flow west and north are swifter because of the steeper gradient and their clear and sparkling waters reveal the stones which form their beds. The chief of these streams is the River Nar which flows past Castle Acre, giving its name to Narborough and Narford.

Considering how small most of these rivers are it is surprising how many watermills there are upon them. In Domesday Book practically every parish is recorded as having a mill and they were watermills, for windmills were invented later. The parishes which were not on rivers acquired windmills and the rest often supplemented the existing watermills with windmills. At Burnham Overy there are good specimens of both kinds, and both are in an excellent state of preservation. The windmill, dating from 1814, is a tower mill of the most sophisticated design, with the tower solidly built of brick surmounted by a revolving cap, but the machinery has been removed. Wooden post mills date from the thirteenth century and there are few examples, even of very much later date, remaining. Watermills in Norfolk are in almost every instance of the undershot type in which the wheels are driven by water flowing under them and pushing the paddles forwards and upwards; whereas overshot mills, which can be found in more hilly parts of the country, are driven by water falling on to the wheels and forcing the paddles downwards by its weight. This method requires a head of water which cannot usually be obtained in Norfolk.

In addition to mills for grinding corn there were many, both in the Fens and on the Broads, which were used for drainage purposes. Some of these are still to be seen between Acle and Great Yarmouth. The sails of these windmills, through a series of gears, turned, what were in effect, water wheels in reverse, for they scooped water out of one channel and lifted it into another at a higher level through which it could flow to the sea. Wind power gave way to steam in the early nineteenth century and steam in turn gave way to diesel engines in the twentieth century, but in the Fens the old engine houses, sometimes with their tall chimneys, can still be seen. Many old watermills have been preserved by being adapted for private houses, but windmills are not so convenient for this purpose. In Norfolk a great many other buildings which might have been lost have been saved by conversion into private houses. Country inns, railway stations and village schools have come on to the market in numbers, together with country rectories which no longer house the clergy, and all these help to maintain the former appearance of the countryside.

A growing number of Norfolk villages have a village sign standing in some prominent position and it will be obvious at a glance that most of them come from the same source. They are carved in wood and the subject matter is some scene from the history of the place or some person or emblem associated with it. The first three of these signs were erected on the Royal estate by order of King George v in 1912, and were designed by Mr A. Kingston Rudd and made in the Queen's carving school at Sandringham; but the majority have been carved by Mr H. Carter of Swaffham, where he first made a sign showing the Pedlar whose story is told elsewhere in this book. He has since made many of these colourful additions to the village scene. They are worth a pause for examination as they are not only informative but are evidence that the local people who have had them erected take a pride in the village in which they live.

The climate, wide skies and the wealth of natural subjects have provided inspiration to artists from the birth of the Norwich School of painting in the time of the 'Old Crome' until the present day. There is so much to inspire the painter and the weather allows him to paint out of doors at his leisure. There are the great trees and the cottages which inspired Crome; the wild flowers and plants and the village churches which Cotman depicted; and the artists of the present day have found many more subjects in the old buildings and the patterns made during the construction of new ones, the birds and the wide skies of the salt marshes. The sailing craft on the beaches a century ago have given way to other types of boats, or the pattern made by wreckage; and in some cases an artist has taken a very limited subject, such as the view from his own house, and painted it from every angle and in various lights. Norwich prides itself on having had the only school of painting in England, in the sense that the schools of the Continent were given that name. The

Introduction

Norwich School derived much inspiration from the Dutch painters and flourished during the first 30 or 40 years of the nineteenth century, but its influence persists. Norfolk seems to be full of artists, both professional and amateur, and many of them rise to national fame. Sir Alfred Munnings, although born in Suffolk, worked for some time in Norwich, Edward Seago has also achieved great popularity, and many others working in the present day produce work which is esteemed locally if not farther afield.

If Norfolk provides favourable conditions for artists to work it must also suit authors, for there are many who find peace and inspiration here. Diarists and letter writers always seem to have abounded, from the time of the Pastons in the early fifteenth century, whose letters provide such a colourful picture of life in that period. Parson Woodforde, in the latter half of the eighteenth century, kept his famous diary, which gives such intimate details of life in a country parish, and he was followed by Victorian country parsons and others who were sometimes concerned with a wider canvas. The best-loved story about horses which has ever been written, *Black Beauty*, was by Anna Sewell, who was born at Yarmouth and lived in Norwich. I once met an elderly woman who could remember the horses which are mentioned in the story. Sir Henry Rider Haggard, author of *King Solomon's Mines* and other popular stories of Africa, was a Norfolk man who finally settled at Ditchingham where his daughter, Lilias Rider Haggard carried on the tradition by writing books about Norfolk life. For a time, Henry Williamson lived and farmed in Norfolk, and R. H. Mottram, who became famous when his book about the 1914-18 war, *The Spanish Farm*, was published, was a Norwich man who became its chief citizen when he was honoured by being chosen to be Lord Mayor. He continued to write innumerable novels including one, entitled *Our Mr Dormer*, which was set in the head office of Gurney's bank of which his father was manager. There are numerous other authors, many of them still writing, too numerous to mention, who are Norfolk born or who have settled in the county; and besides books of general interest there is a steady stream of books about specialized aspects of Norfolk life or history, whole volumes about the history of individual towns, or, like the well-named *Victorian Miniature* by Professor Owen

Chadwick, who spends much of his time in Norfolk, the story of a tiny parish of less than 250 inhabitants over a period of about 30 years. Norfolk has provided settings for detective and mystery stories—lonely marshes seem to provide an ideal locale for adventure stories for young and old, as have also the Broads. So much has been written that, in addition to the huge collection of material relating to the county in Norwich Central Library's Colman and Rye collections, there are thousands of books in its store-rooms which have some mention of the county, albeit small, whether they happen to be works of fact or fiction.

The theatre has always flourished in Norfolk. St George's Guildhall at King's Lynn was a theatre in Shakespeare's time and he is said to have acted there. After some years as a warehouse for scenery, it was restored and plays and concerts now take place in it again. A theatre existed in the early eighteenth century a few feet from the west end of St Peter Mancroft Church in Norwich and this in turn was superseded by the Theatre Royal in 1757. The first Theatre Royal was destroyed by fire and was followed by another building on the same site in 1826, and again after another fire by the present building in 1936. Parson Woodforde visited the theatre from time to time, though this involved staying in Norwich for the night. The present Theatre Royal is one of the few in England capable of supporting top-ranking touring companies. In addition, since the 1920s, Norwich has supported an almost unique theatrical venture which has become world famous—the Maddermarket Theatre, founded by Nugent Monck—which, with amateur actors and professional producers and designers, has achieved a high standard of performance and has presented every Shakespeare play and the classics from Aristophanes through every age and country to Pinter and Brecht. Nugent Monck started his company in the Music House, one of the oldest buildings in Norwich, which at one time housed the city's Waites—performers and mummers who took part in civic pageants. When Queen Elizabeth I visited Norwich she was entertained by a masque in the garden at the rear of what is now the Strangers' Club in Elm Hill, but the proceedings were spoiled by rain. Acting evidently has deep roots in Norfolk. In the market towns and even in a number of villages, dramatic and operatic activities flourish, for the people who live at a distance from the larger centres are well able to provide their own entertainment.

The county was once covered with a network of meandering railway lines run by two competing companies: the Great Eastern Railway and the Midland and Great Northern Joint Railway. The latter was one of the first complete systems in the country to be closed in the 1950s. It ran from Great Yarmouth to Leicester with a number of branch lines and had its headquarters at Melton Constable. The competition was such that most of the market towns and villages in the northern half of the county had either two stations or alternative routes to choose from, but now the main lines of the old Great Eastern Railway to Norwich, Great Yarmouth and King's Lynn are almost all that remain. The railway enthusiast will find that everything possible has been recorded about the old M. & G.N.R. and he will be able to trace the embankments and cuttings if he wishes. We can, however, enjoy what remains. The railway from Norwich to Cambridge passes through some pleasant country; first through farm land and then, after leaving Attleborough, it enters the Breckland, which is at its best between Thetford and Brandon where the train winds through the forest, following the course of the Little Ouse river which can be seen from time to time through the trees. The main line from Norwich to London is less varied and reaches the county boundary sooner, passing through farming country of small irregularly shaped fields. In general, the view from the train has changed little during the past 50 years. Modern machinery appears in the fields, but it completes its task and quickly disappears again leaving the ploughed soil, the sprouting seed, the ripening grain, which in the larger fields assume for a time the same tint and light and shade as the wide stretches of sand left clean and untrodden by the retreating tide on the Norfolk coast.

The combine harvesters appear, the stubble is full of pheasants for a few days and then the whole cycle of ploughing and cultivation starts again. People working in the fields pause to wave to the train as it passes just as they have done ever since trains began, and, shades of the *Railway Children*, a toot from the driver's horn brings a group of children to the bottom of a cottage garden to wave a greeting. When the land has been ploughed, the variety of colour in the soil is surprising. It ranges from black through every shade of brown to white and in places it is red. This is due to a complex pattern of surface soils which sometimes vary even in the same field.

The architecture of a district is largely influenced by the building materials which are available, and most of Norfolk is singularly lacking in stone. However, in such a large county with regions differing in nature, such as the Marshland in the west, the higher arable land, heath, forest and coast, there is a corresponding difference in the styles of building. In much of the county there is no predominant style. In the past most cottages and farm houses were timber-framed with a filling of wattle and daub, and there was also 'clay lump'. This consisted of rectangular blocks of clay mixed with straw, coarse grass and occasionally pieces of flint, which were made on the spot and air-dried, jointed with puddled clay. Provided that the roof, which was frequently thatched with Norfolk reed, was sound and had projecting eaves, and the walls were colour washed or painted with tar, the building would last for years, but once the roof was gone disintegration would be rapid. Clay lump was easy to alter. If a window or door was needed a suitable hole could be easily made in the wall. The fashion for converting cottages into 'desirable residences' reached Norfolk just too late to save many of these timber-framed houses which had been allowed to stand empty and fall into ruin, so the scenery has been the loser.

It was probably due to the fact that the agricultural population of Norfolk was at its peak about 1850 that so many of the cottages and farmhouses in central and west Norfolk are uninteresting architecturally. They are usually brick boxes with no attempt at ornamentation or style, yellow brick in the western side of the county and red brick in most other parts. The part of the county which has a distinctive, predominant style is in the north, particularly near the coast, for here flint is everywhere, with curved red or black pantiles for the roofs. Rounded flint pebbles could be picked off the beaches, and irregularly shaped flints abounded on the surface of the fields where flint picking was quite an industry, not only for building but for road making as well. Many of the pantiles are supposed to have come from Holland as ballast in the small ships which traded from Wells, Blakeney and other small ports. Building with pebbles was most comomn near the coast and the flints from the fields were either used as they were, or split with the flat side facing outwards. Some of the tiles were made locally so that the houses were of local materials and contributed towards the unity of the scene. There is something memorable in the pattern of black or grey walls and red tiles when seen in the light reflected from the wide sky, sometimes against grey clouds over the sea behind.

In west Norfolk there is a belt of building stone called carstone, which extends from Downham Market to Hunstanton, and there are sufficient buildings of this material to give a special character to the area. Carstone, a brown sandstone, hardens upon exposure to the air and the colour reminds one of the gingerbread house in the story of Hansel and Gretel. Though sometimes employed in blocks, it is often used in flat pieces with the narrow edges showing. When the building is of blocks of stone, the joints are often 'galletted', which means that small pieces of stone, usually not larger than an inch across, are inserted in the wide mortar joints, giving a decorative appearance. This style of building can be seen particularly well at Hunstanton and Sandringham. At Thetford, Stoke Ferry and other parts of west Norfolk, some of the harder chalk is used for building, but no attempt has been made to add decoration. I do not want to give the impression that Norfolk is lacking in beautiful old cottages —this is far from the truth—but they are scattered and do not form such charming groups as in some other districts. One may come across some which remind one of a painting by Constable or Cotman, and there is still a great deal of thatch and whitewash.

The majority of churches in the county are constructed either in whole or in part from flint. The proportion of limestone used, acts as a guide to the wealth of the builder. Norwich Cathedral is entirely of Caen stone imported from Normandy; and in the Marshland stone was brought from Northamptonshire by water; but some of the simpler village churches have little or no stone and sometimes the dressings are of brick. One reason why round towers were attached to so many of the smaller churches may have been the fact that they required no corner stones and could be constructed entirely of locally picked flints. At Framingham Earl and some other examples, the corner stones of the nave are actually very large blocks of flint.

In the particular group of churches to which Framingham Earl belongs it is the fine Norman doorways which are of stone, but there is little other stone of early date in them.

Norfolk villages vary in character and plan, not surprisingly in such a large county. There are good examples of the 'street' plan, such as at Long Stratton where houses and shops extend for nearly a mile along either side of the main road. There are villages in the same neighbourhood, such as Mellis or Fritton, which surround a large village green or common, others like Heydon are built round a small compact village green, but very many have no plan at all, no focal point of any kind. I live in such a place. The church is isolated, with no houses, except for one farm, anywhere near it. The post office, village pub, the two shops and the village hall are all at some distance from each other. The school is actually on the parish boundary about a mile from the centre of the inhabited area, and is a few hundred yards from the nearest houses, if the two adjoining ones which are in the next parish are ignored. The vicarage is half a mile, as the crow flies, from the church and a mile by road from most of the village. I do not suggest that this lack of planning is typical, but there do seem to be a great many villages in the county which are like this example. The Black Death is frequently blamed for the isolation of many of the churches, for the villages were destroyed to prevent infection and rebuilt on fresh sites. The decline in the rural population since 1850 and the increase in certain villages by an influx of town dwellers has resulted in houses being built on sites not previously used for building. A number of factors varying from place to place have influenced the plan of each village. Many have the air of being tiny towns, and in fact had markets at one time. Places like Banham, East Harling, Cawston and Worstead are among these. A glance at *White's Directory of Norfolk* (1845) shows that these places supported trades and professions which would be inconceivable today. They have tiny market places round which are grouped shops, and houses which obviously were once shops, as well as former inns. First the railways and then buses enabled the people to visit larger towns for their requirements and now the private car continues to draw people away. The number of people working on the land is fewer by far than it was. One or two men equipped with

10 *Norwich Castle (c. 1160), refaced 1833-39*

tractors can farm the land more efficiently than the bands of labourers who did so until early in the twentieth century, frequently aided by the women and children.

Norfolk is a naturalist's paradise. Not only are there bird sanctuaries, like the one at Scolt Head, where bird watching can be pursued, but there is the teeming life of the Broads, where in spite of the holiday traffic, there are still many secluded places where rare birds, butterflies and plants flourish. The bird watcher and the botanist find ample material for their interests and the number of books which have been written and illustrated testify to the opportunities which present themselves to professional and amateur. Sea birds are present in large numbers, flying out to their feeding grounds and returning at dusk. The migrants may be seen too as they leave or arrive on their journeys to and from Europe. Seals breed on the sandbanks of the Wash and off Great Yarmouth. All over Norfolk the hedgerows and lokes (the Norfolk word for drove, bridle path, twitten or whatever it is called in other parts of the country) harbour many living things. A drive along a country road is a series of near misses as pheasants seem to wait until the very last moment before taking off from under the wheels in their ungainly way, and families of these birds sit on railway lines, not even troubling to fly when they make their last-minute escape. It is sad that the number of hedgehogs which fail to complete their journeys across roads is large, but rats are more nimble, though many are killed. Myxamytosis appeared to have exterminated the rabbit population, but they are returning in increasing numbers. Hares, which escaped the disease, may frequently be seen racing across the fields, and sometimes leap the roadside hedges. The red squirrel can sometimes still be seen, the grey squirrel has become established in the forest area, and moles, stoats, mice and voles abound. Unfortunately coypu, which were introduced for their fur, escaped and became a pest in Broadland. Vigorous methods are being employed to try to exterminate them but without complete success. They undermine the banks of rivers and could lead to flooding if left to their own devices. Sailing or drifting quietly along a river one wonders how many little eyes are watching from the holes near the waterline and from the banks. At night an owl may be discovered in a tree overhead quietly watch-

11   *Norwich Cathedral: Norman tower and late fifteenth-century spire from the cloisters*

ing with its head rotating on a motionless body until it finally flies away, so silently for its size. In spring the call of the cuckoo becomes a pest. Moorhens turn up from nowhere as soon as a pond fills with water, and I have seen some herons frequenting a pond in the middle of a field until all the water had evaporated. The country dweller in Norfolk is close to nature, sometimes he has to battle with it for self-preservation, but on the whole nature gives more than she takes.

Norfolk has been inhabited by man for about 400,000 years. At first man lived and hunted during the inter-glacial periods when the ice of the Ice Ages retreated northwards; his flint tools of the Old Stone Age have been found at Whitlingham, south of Norwich, in a condition as fresh as when they were made. In that immensely long period in early man's history, the inhabitants were few and progress slow, but when the New Stone Age, or Neolithic Period, began about 8,000 B.C. the population increased and left many traces of its existence, of which Grimes Graves is an outstanding example. From that time onwards Norfolk has always been populated, for the earliest record, Domesday Book, which gives the state of affairs in 1065, shows it to be the most populous part of England, and so it remained until the Industrial Revolution in the eighteenth century. In the same way Norwich, its capital, was at times the second largest city in England, rivalled only by Bristol, until the use of coal and steam led to the rise of the industrial cities of the Midlands and the North.

Norfolk's main industry has been the only industry which is really vital to mankind—agriculture—but from the earliest times there has been a growing number of industries. The neolithic flint mines supplied the raw material for the makers of flint tools and implements. The Bronze Age, which followed, has left plenty of evidence that bronze tools, weapons and ornaments of all kinds were made here; there are no raw materials on the spot, but scrap metal was used to manufacture them. These Bronze Age people also made pottery, including urns in which they buried the cremated remains of their dead, and 250 of their barrows, or burial mounds, have been found scattered fairly evenly over the county. About A.D. 500 immigrants from the continent of Europe brought the knowledge of iron tools and weapons, few of which have remained, but there are ample traces of their presence in the form of pottery and sites of their habitations, including that of a fairly complete farmstead which has been discovered at Micklemoor Hill near East Harling. About 300 B.C. there was an invasion of warriors from the Marne district of France, who, among other things, introduced chariots for warlike purposes. They must have been superior to the earlier Iron Age people, not only in military but in artistic ability, judging from articles which have been discovered. The Marnians were overcome in turn by the Belgae, who came from eastern France and Belgium and are familiar to every schoolboy who has 'done' Caesar. But although the Belgae conquered most of south-east England they failed to penetrate into Norfolk, which remained independent under a tribe called the Iceni. Even in Roman times there was a degree of self government in the area and the officials at Venta Icenorum (the market of the Iceni) were probably Romanized Britons. Some of the most spectacular archaeological remains which have been unearthed in Norfolk date from the Marnian period. They include the famous Snettisham treasures of gold alloy and bronze torcs, or neck ornaments, and other ornaments which show the wealth and artistic ability of these people. The Belgae had introduced coinage into the country and some of this was minted locally. Vivid dioramas showing typical scenes of life in each of the periods already mentioned may be seen at Norwich Castle Museum together with examples of flint implements, pottery, bronze and iron tools and weapons, and gold and other ornaments which have been discovered in the county. Here also are many types of objects from the Roman occupation which lasted for nearly 400 years.

Soon after the Romans came, the Iceni rose under the leadership of their Queen Boadicea, and succeeded in sacking Camulodunum (Colchester), but in the end the Romans put down the rebellion. The impressive site of Venta Icenorum, which can still be seen at Caister-by-Norwich, is by no means the only evidence of Roman occupation to be seen in the county. Caister-by-Sea to the north of Great Yarmouth, has been excavated and the lay-out of part of the Roman town can be seen, and there is the impressive, imperishable fortress of Burgh Castle guarding Breydon Water, albeit on the Suffolk bank. A good deal of evidence of farming activity has been unearthed in the region, but although agriculture flourished in Norfolk under the Romans, industries were established as well and at Caister-by-Norwich glass was manufactured and it was believed that there was a woollen industry there. Iron was smelted in west Norfolk where the greensand yielded ore, and pottery was made upon a commercial basis as, for instance, at Morley St Peter. Roman villas which have been discovered in Norfolk are not the more luxurious type sometimes found in other parts of Britain, but the homes of farmers. Many modern roads in Norfolk have been made on foundations laid by the Romans, some of them minor roads in addition to the main routes. The pattern of modern Norfolk was beginning to emerge, for parish boundaries often follow the lines of Roman roads. These parish boundaries were settled by the Saxons in the ninth or tenth century and so too were the boundaries of other administrative areas. The Angles and the Saxons began to settle before the Romans left, in A.D. 425. These early settlers came by arrangement with the Romans to help defend the country against other raiding Angles and Saxons, but as soon as the Romans left their towns and villas were deserted and large numbers of raiding Angles and Saxons settled in the county, penetrating inland up the river valleys. Within a hundred years they were well established and the Kingdom of East Anglia had come into being. They soon became known as the North Folk and the South Folk, who occupied modern Norfolk and Suffolk respectively. The counties were divided into districts called hundreds, each with its own court. In vain will one look for places named Launditch, Humbleyard or Henstead, for instance, but these names of former hundreds are perpetuated in the titles of rural districts and rural deaneries of today.

East Anglia was on the defensive, both from invasion from the sea where it was constantly being attacked by Norsemen who succeeded in settling in many places which bear Danish names to this day, and from attack by the Mercians who lived in the Midlands. The Fens provided a natural obstacle on the western side of Norfolk, but attack was possible along the Icknield Way, that great prehistoric trackway which linked Norfolk with the South West via Newmarket and Royston. Great earthworks and ditches were built near Newmarket, and Thetford Castle defended the spot where the road crossed the Rivers Thet and Little Ouse.

Although Christian East Anglia failed to prevent domination by the pagan Mercians who invaded it in the seventh century, it was allowed to maintain self-government in much the same way as it did during Roman times, but it failed to keep out the Danes.

Christianity had been introduced into East Anglia by A.D. 617 by St Felix, after whom Felixstowe is named. He established himself at Dunwich on the Suffolk coast. Very soon, in A.D. 673, a separate bishopric was established at North Elmham in Norfolk. The first Cathedral there, like most churches of the period, was doubtless made of wood. It was a period when people did not build permanent buildings. Lord Clark, in his book *Civilization*, has suggested that this was so because of a lack of confidence in the future. One of the contributory reasons for this attitude was the belief in the predictions of the Book of Revelation that the world would come to an end at the Millennium—the year 1000. When this date was safely passed, there was a wave of building in permanent building materials. Not only were hundreds of village churches erected in Norfolk alone, but a stone cathedral was built at North Elmham, extensive remains of which can still be seen, and in 1065 there were already at least 25 churches in Norwich.

The Norman Conquest accelerated the urge to build, for the Normans had boundless energy. Norwich Cathedral was started in 1094 and was already sufficiently complete in five years for it to be used, though it is probable that it was 80 years before it was finished. In addition to the large number of parish churches in the county which have some Norman work in them were the great priory churches of Wymondham, Castle Acre, Binham and Thetford. The great castles of Norwich, Castle Rising and Castle Acre, also date from the same period. Notable Norman parish churches are South Lopham, Walsoken, Hales and Heckingham, to quote examples from widely scattered parts of the county. The wealth of church architecture, particularly that of the fifteenth century, bears witness to the prosperity of the region which was the centre of the cloth-making industry in the Middle Ages. Wealthy merchants married into the gentry and acquired country estates, so starting the habit of living in the country while having business interests in the city, which has continued to this day. The ports of Great Yarmouth and King's Lynn grew prosperous through trading with the Continent; the Wars of the Roses and the Civil War passed the county by, except for the siege of King's Lynn by the Parliamentarians which was of short duration, so that trade and daily life were not disrupted by war. Plague and diseases were the greatest setbacks, the Black Death of 1348-9 killing off possibly one-third of the population. The daily life of Norfolk in the fifteenth century has been described in the *Paston Letters* and that of the second half of the eighteenth century in James Woodforde's *Diary of a Country Parson*. Since Woodforde's day many other diaries have added a personal touch to the masses of official records.

If we were transported back into the past we would find landmarks which would be recognizable; the mill would be where one was when Domesday Book was compiled, the church would be on the same site, though altered and enlarged or rebuilt through the centuries, but little changed since the early sixteenth century. The minor roads, though better surfaced, would otherwise look much as they did, with their twists and turns dictated centuries ago by the boundaries of property. The manor houses, many of them with their moats, would be there too, but the country vicarages and rectories which have long been a feature of the scene, would not have been there in most cases before the early part of the nineteenth century. The predecessor of one of these Victorian rectories in which I lived for a time, was described as a 'poor cottage'. Such a parsonage can be seen opposite the church at Ketteringham—a small black-and-white cottage which is probably in a better condition now than it ever was. The mid-Victorian Vicar lived in a far more imposing house some distance away at Hethersett. All these things are part of old England which, in Norfolk, has evolved slowly, and still evolves. The wisdom of long experience in the art of living does not take kindly to enthusiasts who would make sweeping changes. It wears them down so that in the end it is the innovators who are changed.

CHAPTER TWO

Norwich

The traveller to Norwich should approach, if possible, by the New-market Road. From London a choice of routes converge. All use the A.11 for the last 50 miles of the journey and this is likewise the best approach from the West and the South Midlands. Much of the road runs through pleasant country. One feels that one is in East Anglia as soon as one leaves Baldock by the road to Royston and after the Norfolk boundary is reached the countryside is marred only by recent development at Thetford. The road through Thetford Chase is beautiful, but between Attleborough and Wymondham the scenery of the boulder clay region is less interesting; and between Hether-sett and Cringleford the countryside is open with large undulating fields. It is wise to stop at Wymondham, a pleasant market town with historic buildings and some interesting features described else-where in this book. At Cringleford one crosses a narrow stone bridge 600 years old and suddenly one is in Norwich.

The complete change from country to city can also be experienced where the road from Watton crosses the River Yare at Earlham and where it is also crossed by the road from Ipswich at Harford Bridge, for this river has formed the western and southern boundary of the city of Norwich ever since its limits were fixed in 1556. It was not till 400 years later that the boundary was revised and the in-habitants of Cringleford and Thorpe successfully resisted attempts to include them in the orbit of Norwich. Ribbon development has not taken place along these three approaches to the city. Once inside the boundary, the Newmarket Road provides one of the most beautiful approaches a city could have. Even a Cambridge writer admitted that Trumpington Road there was rivalled by Newmarket Road, Norwich. For over a mile, the straight road is lined with fine trees through which the sunlight pours more often than not and, behind the trees, some of the best houses in the city stand in well-kept gardens. The last, and older section of the road is wider and the Victorian houses in their large gardens stand among mature trees; it is probably even more beautiful than the more formal newer section of the road, which has already been traversed. After this fine approach, it is unfortunate that the continuation is along St Stephen's Street, a post-war development which is like a popular shopping centre in any other town; but this is not typical of Norwich. The charm of Norwich lies rather in the city enclosed by the medieval walls, and its treasures have to be looked for, for it is part of the Norfolk temperament not to advertise. Norwich has much to offer and is supremely well-worth seeing, but it is not a contrived showplace, it is not commercialized; it is just what it has developed into in the course of centuries and it is how its inhabitants like it to be.

The only occasion upon which I visited Norwich before I came to live in Norfolk, was for half a day in the 1930s. I went to the Cathedral, had tea in Tombland, climbed the Castle Mound and returned home convinced that I had seen everything there was to see. I have since encountered visitors who have had much the same impression. I did not see, or even know of, the real centre of the city, and the motorist who passes through will be in the same position as I was. Even the visitor on foot will not see the charms of the place unless guided, and verbal directions are almost impossible to follow, for the city is a network of narrow streets and passages.

I have brought the reader to the capital of East Anglia, and I really mean that, for Norwich is not just the county town of Norfolk, but a real regional capital and centre, whether bureaucrats like it or not. It is the largest city within a radius of one hundred miles, though in respect of population it is challenged by the growth of Ipswich. But Ipswich has not the poise of Norwich; size is not the only criterion of importance. In East Anglia, things tend to be more important in proportion to their size than the stranger would suspect, and this certainly applies to Norwich. Do not underrate it because its population is only round about 120,000. It has the amenities and importance lacking in cities three times its size.

It took me a month to find my way about the centre of Norwich. Although the Cathedral has one of the highest spires in the country, its situation is so low-lying that it cannot be seen from many of the streets. The Castle dominates the city and the streets go round it. After all, its builders in the time of William the Conqueror placed it where it is so that it should block the main road. The real focal point is the old Saxon market place, Tombland, and the 17 roads which lead to Norwich from every point of the compass once met there. Norwich is a place which people come *to*—for trade, shopping, entertainment, great occasions, for legal business and much else besides. They have been doing so for a thousand years. Two of the chief reasons which draw people from every part of Norfolk to Norwich are the Cathedral, where representatives from the 600 parishes in the Diocese meet together on several occasions in the year for special services or meetings, and Norwich City Football Club, which can draw crowds which other league clubs would envy. When, as sometimes happens, fixtures for both these attractions clash, there is chaos in the streets.

Norwich, contrary to the stranger's preconceived idea, is a hilly place. The old road, known as Ber Street, which brings in much of the city's food from the market gardens and farms to the south-east, is probably of Roman origin. It runs along the top of a ridge which drops steeply down to the part of the River Wensum which serves as a port for sea-going vessels and has done so since the bank at this point became the first settlement in Saxon times. King Street was the main street of this settlement, and the oldest house in the city, now part of Wensum Lodge, is to be found there, as well as the remains of Carrow Abbey, three churches and a number of other ancient buildings including Howard House which was the home of the family of that name before they became Dukes of Norfolk. Although it is not obvious, the ancient line followed by King Street continues through Tombland and over Fye Bridge and up Magdalen Street northwards, following a route over 1,000 years old.

Beyond the Cathedral rises Mousehold Heath, made famous by the painter 'Old Crome', and by George Borrow, who said of the view: 'A fine city, truly, is that, view from whatever side you will: but it shows best from the east, where ground, bold and elevated, overlooks the fair and fertile valley in which it stands. Gazing from these heights, the eye beholds a scene which cannot fail to awaken, even in the least sensitive bosom, feelings of pleasure and admiration. At the foot of the heights flows a narrow and deep river, with an antique bridge communicating with a long and narrow suburb, flanked on either side by rich meadows of the brightest green, beyond which spreads the city; the fine old city, perhaps the most curious specimen at present extant of the genuine old English town.' The bridge to which he refers dates from the thirteenth century, and the meadow is now the playing field of Norwich School. Although written in 1851, what Borrow said is still true.

It is within the past decade that the Cattle Market which had been held on the steep hill below the Castle walls for 300 years, and was one of the largest markets in the country, was moved to the outskirts of the city. Not only did the market bring business to the city in the old days, it provided a great deal of entertainment and was a weekly reminder that the prosperity of Norwich came primarily from the soil. Droves of animals still arrived through the city streets, doubtless to the annoyance of the motorists who were made to feel their lesser importance in the scheme of things. However, the motorist has been defeated in Norwich; the pedestrian has ousted cars from its main shopping street and several other narrow streets besides, so that shopping can be done in safety and in greater quiet. The loudest sound in these streets now is the clatter of footsteps.

The origin of Norwich is obscure, but there is no direct evidence of its being earlier than Saxon times, although the Roman road from Caister which ran along the line of Ber Street probably crossed the river near Bishop Bridge. Northwic (*wic* means a settlement) was the name given to the village which grew up on the bank of the river at the foot of the ridge along which Ber Street runs and this name ultimately became that of the whole group including Westwic, the district inside the city gate to the west. Coslany was an early settlement on the north bank of the River Wensum and was always regarded as part of the city. St Mary's Coslany Church has a round Saxon tower with typical double windows with triangular heads. It is the oldest Church in Norwich, though St John Timberhill, near the Castle, has some Saxon long-and-short work at its north-east corner.

Norwich had become sufficiently important by A.D. 925 to have a mint, and coins were struck here from the reign of King Athelstan about that time, until about 1250. After an interval of 200 years the mint was re-opened for two months from July 1465 in the reign of Edward IV, and again from 1696 to 1697 in the reign of William III. The town grew rapidly and by 1065 had a population of about 5,500 and there were 25 churches. A castle was built here within a few months of the Norman Conquest and a French Colony was started. A new market place was created where the present one is, while the old Saxon market continued at Tombland until it died out through competition from the newer one. In 1094 the building of the Cathedral was begun and the completed portion was consecrated in 1101. The present stone Castle was built about 1160, by which time there was a strong colony of Jews, who had come from Normandy. The twelfth-century house of Jurnet and his son Isaac is incorporated in Wensum Lodge, King Street, formerly known as the Music House. Unusually complete records of the community have been found and the sites of the houses owned by Jews in White Lion Street can be identified. In 1144 the Jews were accused of murdering a boy named William, who was afterwards regarded as a saint, but they were able to obtain protection from the King's representatives. The incident has been investigated by M. D. Anderson in her book *A Saint at Stake* and her conclusions make its authenticity dubious.

Norwich was an important manufacturing centre from medieval times, with 130 recorded trades in the thirteenth century— diversification much as it is today. In addition, there was a great deal of foreign trade with the Continent. This state of affairs continued for centuries until the industrial revolution, which passed Norwich by— fortunately perhaps, for the wealth of old buildings and gardens and the close proximity to the countryside would have been lost if expansion had taken place in the nineteenth century. The city walls, which were begun in 1294 and finished in 1320, enclosed an area of a square mile, exactly the same size as that of the City of London. Additional walls and towers were erected in 1342 at the expense of

Richard Spynke, a wealthy citizen. All the city gates were demolished at the end of the eighteenth century, but some extensive stretches of the walls and some of the towers remain. Although there are a number of fine eighteenth-century houses within the city walls, there are no eighteenth-century squares and terraces as in London, Bristol or Exeter, for little or no development took place outside the walls until the end of the eighteenth century; but the outer boundaries, fixed when it was made a separate county from Norfolk in 1403 in the reign of Henry VI, remained much the same for 560 years, and still follow the original line on the western, southern and eastern sides, nearly 14 miles in circumference.

In the course of history many kings and queens have visited the city; there have been uprisings, in the thirteenth century due to friction between the monks of the Benedictine Priory and the townspeople, and in 1381, when 50,000 rebels, protesting against the Poll Tax assembled in Norfolk, were defeated by Bishop Henry de Spencer, who had been trained as a soldier. Perhaps the most famous attack on the city was on the occasion of Kett's Rebellion in 1549, when 20,000 rebels led by Robert Kett, a tanner, and his brother, William, a butcher, both of Wymondham, encamped on Mousehold Heath and attacked the city. The rebellion was defeated and the two ringleaders were executed.

Norwich suffered from the Black Death of 1348-9 as severely as anywhere, and suffered also from plagues at frequent intervals caused by overcrowding and insanitary conditions. These conditions continued well into the nineteenth century when there were still serious epidemics. In spite of this, Norwich, as well as the rest of Norfolk, has been noted for the longevity of its citizens.

Like its nearest neighbours, Ely and Peterborough, the Cathedral is basically a Norman building, but unlike them it has not been altered much in later periods, so that we can see its plan as it was intended in the first instance. It retains the round apse which was the fashion in buildings of its period, in the centre of which, facing west, is a Saxon Bishop's throne, the only one of its kind remaining in such a position in northern Europe. The interior is remarkably clean and light in spite of the massive Norman arcades. The triforium arches are the same height as those below them in the nave, and above the clerestory is the chief addition to the original nave: the stone vaulting added nearly 400 years later, with its hundreds of coloured and gilded bosses. Roof bosses are one of the great features at Norwich. There are more than 2,000 in all, those in the cloisters being of great interest and easy to study. In the south and west walks they depict incidents in the book of Revelation. The cloisters are probably the finest in England and in their present form took 130 years to build, the work commencing at the north-east corner and progressing in a clockwise direction. The choir stalls belong to the latter part of the fifteenth century. There are a number of medieval paintings on wood, which in England are a rarity owing to the wholesale destruction during the Reformation and Commonwealth. In this present more enlightened age, restoration and beautifying the building is the concern of those who have the care of it, and it is probably used more for large services than at any time in its history. In comparison with other churches of its size the number of monuments is few, but outside the east end of the Cathedral is the grave of Nurse Edith Cavell, who is still remembered for her courage when facing a German firing squad in Belgium in 1915.

The Cathedral Close, which is divided into two sections known as the Upper and Lower Close, is best visited in the evening, or on a Saturday or Sunday when the numerous offices housed in the old houses are closed and there are consequently fewer cars and people about. All the houses are carefully maintained, whether used as private residences or offices, and the Cathedral dominates the whole scene. There is the real atmosphere of a cathedral close, enhanced by contrast with the busy city outside. Some of the houses incorporate remains of the monastic buildings which lost their original uses at the Dissolution of the Monasteries. Others date from the seventeenth and eighteenth centuries. In the Lower Close, the south side consists of a row of Georgian brick houses, the east belongs to the latter half of the seventeenth century and, although built of brick, the houses have a very different appearance; those on the north side are of flint and stand on the site of a monastic brew house. Although differing in materials and date, they all 'live' happily with each other. From the two eastern corners of the Lower Close lead narrow lanes, both lined with houses. That on the south side was once the site of a canal which enabled the builders of the Cathedral to bring the stone to within a few yards of the site by water, after its voyage from Caen in Normandy; in those days a far easier journey than from quarries in some other part of England. Where the canal left the river stands a Tudor water-gate known as Pull's Ferry.

The views of the Cathedral from this part of the river show its great spire rising beyond the playing fields of Norwich School. The lofty spire, 315 feet high, dominates the Cathedral. It was rebuilt in its present form in the latter part of the fifteenth century, replacing a spire which fell a hundred years before, damaging the eastern arm of the building. The result of this damage was the erection of the lovely clerestory of the presbytery, with its graceful flying buttresses, in the 1360s. The spire rises from a massive, but highly decorated Norman tower at the central crossing. The nave is very long, 14 bays, but the effect is somewhat lessened when viewed from inside by the fact that the stone screen surmounted by the organ occupies one bay and the choir stalls occupy the two bays west of the crossing.

Norwich School is an ancient grammar school, which now incorporates the Choir School. The school is watched over by a statue of Nelson, who was a pupil for a time. It is housed in a variety of buildings including the former Bishop's Palace. The School Chapel dates from 1316, and the library is housed in the former private chapel of the Palace.

Outside the confines of the Close, and to the East of the Cathedral, is what at first glance appears to be a large church. But the observer will feel that there is something odd about it and will notice that several chimneys rise from different parts of the roof. The building is in fact the Great Hospital, one of the oldest of such charitable institutions in England and comparable with St Cross at Winchester. Founded in 1256, the charity was re-constituted in the reign of Edward VI and provided lodging for a large number of old people; in fact the eastern and western arms of the church each consist of two storeys divided into cubicles for single men and women. The charity has considerable property and has been able to enlarge the premises from time to time so that married couples have houses of their own.

There is a great hall and a cloister, and the central part of the church serves both as the chapel of the Hospital and the Parish Church of St Helen. There is another much later charity of a somewhat similar type in the city : Doughty's Hospital, in Calvert Street, was founded and endowed by William Doughty who left £6,000 for the purpose in 1687, and this charity too has expanded through wise management.

One of the greatest assets, and liabilities, in Norwich is the incomparable group of ancient churches which survive. In the central area there are 32 medieval churches and two old nonconformist places of worship. Already some of these buildings have been put to secular use, a process which started hundreds of years ago at the time of the Reformation, when the city purchased the huge Dominican Priory Church, now known as St Andrew's Hall, with its chancel, Blackfriars Hall, and has used the former ever since for concerts, exhibitions and so forth. Blackfriars Hall was used as their church for 200 years by Flemish refugees, who settled in Norwich in the time of Elizabeth 1, and by their descendants. After regular services ceased in the eighteenth century, a sermon was preached in Dutch once a year until 1921. St Peter Hungate Church is a museum of ecclesiastical art, and others have been put to different uses, but many are still a problem. Nearly all the churches date from the fifteenth century and some are very fine. The best is St Peter Mancroft, standing on the south side of the market place. It has been regarded as the leading church in the city and has indeed recently officially become so. It is one of the great examples of the Perpendicular style, ashlar-faced with some flushwork decoration, a magnificent roof consisting of hammerbeams encased in a wooden ceiling. Most of the great East window is filled with medieval glass. The canopied font should not be missed and there is a museum at the east end of the building which can be seen upon application. There is a peal of 12 bells in the west tower which is unlike any other in Norwich, possibly because the church was built by the abbey of Gloucester. The building stands on an eminence at the south end of the Market Place. It has always attracted large congregations in spite of having few inhabitants in its parish.

At the opposite end of Bethel Street stands St Giles Church, with a lofty tower which once carried a beacon. It has a light, graceful interior. To the north of St Giles, at the bottom of the ridge upon which it stands, there is a row of ancient churches in St Benedict's Street. St Benedicts' itself was bombed during the last war and only the round tower remains, but within a few hundred yards stand St Swithin, St Lawrence, St Margaret and St Gregory's. Of these the last is the most interesting, with a large painting of St George and the Dragon on one of the west walls. Proceeding eastwards St John Maddermarket, St Andrew's and St Michael at Plea follow in quick succession. St John Maddermarket has more brasses than any other church in Norwich, but unfortunately most of them have been mounted on boards fixed to the walls. St Andrew's is one of the major churches of Norwich, a typical Perpendicular building full of light. It contains a wealth of monuments, including one to Robert Suckling (1589), whose house, Suckling Hall, stands to the east of the church and is used for public functions.

Another group of churches lies over the river in the Coslany ward. They include St George's Colegate, where John Crome worshipped, and St Michael (St Miles) Coslany, with some of the finest flint flush-work to be seen anywhere. St Mary Coslany has a round tower with unmistakable Saxon double windows. John Sell Cotman was baptized here in 1782 and ten years later John Crome was married to Phoebe Berney and in the following year Robert Ladbrooke, a third member of the Norwich School of Painters, was also married in this church. Farther to the east in Pockthorpe is the church of St James, which contains a painted screen with one of the few representations of St Walstan, a Norfolk saint. The boundaries between the parishes are marked in many cases by tablets placed on the walls of houses bearing the initials of the parish and the date. Sometimes there are several tablets together put up at different dates by succeeding churchwardens.

In Theatre Street, close to St Peter Mancroft, is St Stephen's, a very pleasant and interesting church with a number of brasses. As in several of the aforementioned churches, there is no chancel arch in St Stephen's, for the Norwich style of fifteenth-century church building frequently favoured an oblong building with the arcade running the full length of the interior, so that side chapels formed the eastern

12 *Norwich: interior of St Peter Mancroft church*

bays of the aisles. The ecclesiastical list is not complete for Norwich has more medieval churches than any other city and they are part of its character. In some instances, such as St Michael at Plea and St Martin-at-Palace-Plain, they act as focal points of vistas; the church-yards of many of them, which are in the care of the Corporation, are beautifully kept, with flowering trees such as the beautiful range of wisteria at St Giles and the large tree which becomes a mass of white blossom in May in the churchyard of St Andrew's; roses and a camelia bloom outside SS Simon and Jude.

So much rebuilding of churches took place in the fifteenth century that there is a noticeable lack of the Early English and Decorated styles in Norwich. However this is partly remedied by St John's Roman Catholic Church, which dominated the view of the city from the north and west until a block of skyscraper flats competed with it for attention. The building is of cathedral proportions and is a per-fect and scholarly example of the Early English style, entirely ashlar-faced. It was built between 1884 and 1910 at the expense of the Duke of Norfolk and designed by George Gilbert Scott Jnr.

The eighteenth century did not produce any churches in Norwich except the Octagon Chapel in Colegate, and only two or three churches in the whole of Norfolk. What is apparently a Wren church in London Street, Norwich, is a branch of a bank built in 1924. (The genuine eighteenth-century churches are All Saints, North Runcton, in the west of the county, which was probably designed by the King's Lynn architect, Henry Bell, who was responsible for a num-ber of notable buildings; and St Andrew's, Gunton, between North Walsham and Cromer, which was designed by Robert Adam in 1769. St George's, Great Yarmouth, which dated from 1714, has been closed.)

Norwich looks at its best in May when the flowering trees are in blossom. The Cathedral Close is a picture of pink blossom and there are flowering trees in the Castle Gardens and in the numerous church-yards now in the care of the City Parks Department. Close to the centre of the city is a triangular open space known as Chapel Field Gardens, full of flowers and trees. In medieval times the Gardens were part of the property of a large Guild Chapel or chantry which was dissolved at the Dissolution. The site of the Chapel was used in

13   Norwich: old weavers' houses on Elm Hill

the eighteenth century for the Assembly House, designed by Thomas Ivory, a notable local architect. In 1950 the building was thoroughly restored and a trust was created by a local benefactor so that it could be used for cultural purposes. There is a lovely Music Room where local musical societies give concerts; a good and popular restaurant; rooms which are almost always occupied by exhibitions of work by local artists; a small cinema, which is a branch of the National Film Theatre; and other rooms which are in constant use by the many learned societies and other organizations which abound in Norwich.

Next to the Assembly House is the Theatre Royal, the third building of its name to stand on the site. The first theatre in Norwich stood opposite the west front of St Peter Mancroft Church and flourished in the eighteenth century. The first Theatre Royal was built in 1757, also by Ivory, but was burnt down and replaced by another building in 1826. This is turn was destroyed by fire and the present building was erected in 1936. Extensive alterations took place in 1970, and it is now one of the leading theatres in the provinces.

Opposite the Theatre Royal is the central library, a modern building of somewhat grim aspect. But its interior is what matters: purposely it looks inwards to a courtyard in order to avoid the distractions of traffic. Among its contents is a fine collection of books and other material dealing with Norfolk, as well as parish records and other source material. There are facilities for research and for the repair of ancient books and documents, and there are the books which formed the first public library in Norwich, in 1608, which we can imagine Sir Thomas Browne using. His statue sits beside his church, St Peter Mancroft, looking towards the spot where he used to live and where he wrote *Urn Burial* and *Religio Medici*.

The Central Library and its branches are not the only libraries in Norwich, for across the Market Place, behind the fifteenth-century Guildhall, which was completed in 1535 in flint and stone and now serves as the Magistrate's Court, is one of the few subscription libraries surviving in Britain. This institution, of a kind so popular in the late eighteenth and nineteenth centuries and to be found in most fashionable towns, still functions in a pre-1914 club-like atmosphere.

Another reminder of the pre-1914 period is the Royal Arcade which leads off Gentlemen's Walk: the eastern side of the Market

Place. The arcade is a splendid example of Art Nouveau and has fortunately survived almost intact. It was designed in 1899 by the local architect George Skipper, who was responsible for a number of striking Edwardian buildings which survive in Norwich.

On the upper, or west side of the Market Place, stands the imposing City Hall, a commanding building on an excellent site with a tall tower reminiscent of the City Hall at Stockholm. Its great bell can be heard striking the hours almost anywhere in the city. It was built in 1938 and Sir Nikolaus Pevsner considers it to be the finest English public building put up between the wars. A fine range of rooms on the first floor can be thrown into one for civic functions, and a strong-room houses the finest collection of civic plate outside the City of London. If one is fortunate, the Lord Mayor may be seen leaving the City Hall in a state coach drawn by two horses, with bewigged coachman and footmen.

The City Hall dominates the Market Place, which was remodelled and enlarged when it was built, although the site had been in use as a market since Norman times. Dozens of stalls with gaily coloured awnings trade mainly in fruit and vegetables and a variety of other goods.

Opposite the City Hall, looking over the roofs of the shops and offices to the east of the Market Place, is the great Norman Castle, now one of the finest museums in the provinces. Among its many treasures surely the greatest is its collection of paintings of the Norwich School: the only provincial 'school' of painting which has developed in England in the sense that the Italian 'schools' of the Renaissance developed. There is one gallery devoted to a superb collection of pictures by John Sell Cotman, whose water colours are calculated to convert anyone to a love of that medium. Another gallery houses the work of 'Old Crome' and other painters of the Norwich School.

Although the contents of the Cotman and Crome galleries remain fairly constant, the other picture galleries are changed at frequent intervals, with a particular theme for the months in the height of the summer. Mention has already been made of the sections dealing with the archaeology of Norfolk, and there also are rooms dealing with the geology and natural history of the county.

The Castle building itself dates from 1160, although the Normans erected a castle, probably of wood, on the mound shortly after the Conquest. The Keep is 95 feet by 90 feet and 70 feet high, and is unusual as a fortified building in being decorated outside by blank arcading over most of the surface of the walls. The building was completely refaced in 1833-9, but the original features were copied. The buildings which lie at the foot of the Keep date mainly from the period when it was used as the County Gaol; the granite walls surrounding them were built in 1825. The dungeons are shown and there are fine views of the city from the ramparts.

One of the three other museums in Norwich is The Strangers' Hall, one of the most interesting sights in the city. It is a house which has grown through the centuries. There is a thirteenth-century undercroft with a fifteenth-century great hall above, and additions were made in each succeeding century. Some 25 rooms have been furnished in various period styles, including Restoration, Queen Anne, early and late Georgian, Regency and a range of Victorian rooms, as well as a kitchen and exhibits of children's toys and a coach house with a number of vehicles including the Lord Mayor's coach. The great hall is like that of a Cambridge college reduced in size (though it might be truer to say that the halls of the colleges represent large versions of the normal gentlemen's houses of the medieval period.) There is the typical bay on the south side with its tall traceried window, and a gallery at the opposite end over what was once the screens passage.

The Strangers' Hall takes its name from its association with Flemish weavers (strangers to the city), and it should not be confused with the Strangers' Club in Elm Hill. The latter, though housed in a sixteenth-century building once visited by Queen Elizabeth I, is a modern gentlemen's club with a constitution which lays down that a proportion of its members must be strangers, that is, non-natives of Norwich.

Adjoining the Strangers' Hall is the Maddermarket Theatre, a building which has been used variously as a Roman Catholic Church, a Salvation Army Hall and a factory; but in 1926 it was converted by the late Nugent Monck into an Elizabethan-type theatre. Here plays dating from every period and country are produced each month by the Norwich Players, mainly amateur, with a professional producer and designer. It is a highly successful venture from a cultural, educational and entertainment point of view.

The Maddermarket takes its name from the small open space in the road outside the theatre which was once a market where madder roots, the raw materials of a dye, were sold. That was in the days when Norwich was one of the most important cloth-making cities in England. It disputed the place of the second city in England with Bristol, but the rise of the woollen trade in Yorkshire sounded the death knell of the industry. The visitor will notice the parish pump at the lower end of the churchyard (in such a position it was a contributory factor to the epidemics which ravaged the city for centuries and other examples in similar unhygienic positions used to exist).

The citizens of Norwich are proud of their ancient buildings and make every effort to keep them. One street in particular is carefully preserved so as to present somewhat of the appearance of the medieval city and this should not be missed. It is Elm Hill, full of shops carrying on trades carefully selected to harmonize with their setting. It is not a contrived piece, but a live street capable of attracting custom in its own right. The steep gables of some of the buildings of a type which may also be seen in many other parts of the city indicate that these were once the houses of weavers who had their looms in the attic storey with a large window overlooking the street. Part of the charm of this street is its variety. Plaster fronts, each painted in its own colour scheme, are interspersed with timber-framed buildings with brick in-filling such as the Strangers' Club, and either Georgian red-brick or tile-hung fronts which simulate yellow brick. The surface of the street is cobbled with large flint pebbles.

Facing the bottom of Elm Hill stands a very old inn, The Maid's Head, which is medieval in origin although one would never think so from the mock Tudor exterior with its Georgian wing. However, there is an extract from the *Paston Letters* painted on the doors which formed the former main entrance, in which the writer advised a friend to stay at the Maid's Head in 1472. The bedroom in which Queen Elizabeth I is reputed to have slept when she visited Norwich in 1578 is still to be seen. In most places, the Queen would have made sure that she had free hospitality from some wealthy householder, to his financial embarrassment; but the fact that she had to stay at an inn when visiting Norwich gives one food for thought.

Much of the city which lies to the north of the River Wensum is industrial, but there are many old buildings of interest. Colegate has a number of handsome houses and the oldest Congregational church in the country, which was built in 1693. A few doors away is the Octagon Chapel, as we have seen, one of the buildings designed by Thomas Ivory, who also designed the Assembly House. Although this neighbourhood has been used for commercial purposes for a good many years, a start has been made to restore the buildings and make some of them suitable for residence. The 1970s have brought a great change to the area north of Colegate, as much worn-out property has been swept away and a modern shopping centre has taken its place. This has not affected a group of Tudor cottages which face St Augustine's Church and are known as the Gildencroft. The open ground in front of this row of carefully restored houses is the remnant of an open space which was used for recreation by the guilds in medieval times. In Magdalen Street, the main street of 'Norwich over the water', through a narrow archway between two shops, we find an old courtyard called Gurney Court, the appearance of which takes us back a couple of centuries. One of the houses in this quiet little square was the home of the Gurney family at the time when their daughter Elizabeth, later Elizabeth Fry, the Quaker prison reformer, was born in 1780. Another Quaker lady born in Gurney Court in 1802 was Harriet Martineau, who became an author and a pioneer in opening up fresh opportunities for women.

Soon after the birth of Elizabeth, the Gurneys moved to Earlham Hall on the outskirts of Norwich, a seventeenth-century house which now belongs to Norwich Corporation but is leased to the University of East Anglia, after having been used for a variety of other educational purposes for a number of years. Its gardens, which are open to the public, are beautifully kept.

The University of East Anglia, which sprang into life in 1963, is not quite what the people of East Anglia expected when they generously gave large sums of money for its establishment. Of the two parts, the University Village of temporary buildings is probably more pleasant than the permanent buildings, of apparently indestructible concrete on a magnificent site given by the Corporation. It gives the impression of being a factory for turning out graduates. Norwich is not a university city, but a city with a university. Just as it has taken Norwich 900 years to take its Cathedral to its heart, it may take half a millennium to accept the university. Meanwhile the students have to be patient.

Norwich is by no means lacking in enterprise or skill in business, but it does not feel any wish to tell even its own inhabitants what it can do. I remember the chairman of a local business saying, when he heard that a certain item of expenditure was for advertising, 'What do we want to advertise for? Everyone has heard of us.' The same gentleman, when presented with a scheme for taking over a business a few yards over the Suffolk side of the boundary with Norfolk, shook his head and said 'I don't like it. It's not Norfolk.' As events turned out, he was quite right. Norwich and Norfolk are full of enterprise, but it has to be generated from within, not accepted from without just because a thing is a success in London or elsewhere. More than one firm with a well-known name has made the mistake of assuming that it has only to open a branch in Norwich and its name will do the rest. Norwich has beaten them and they have retired sadder, and we hope, wiser. The same sometimes applies to plays which have been running for years and have been a success on tour, but have played to an empty theatre in Norwich. Not that the inhabitants do not fill that theatre or concert hall the following week. They know precisely what they want. For a century Norwich has had a triennial music festival—for its own entertainment; it does not bother to tell the world about it because it has never occurred to it to do so. Such advertising as Norwich has had, has been the result of private enterprise and mainly that of the Norwich Union Insurance Societies. Incorporating the oldest life office in the world, this firm is one of the largest in the country and employs thousands of people at its head office.

Gurney's Bank was one of the chief constituents of Barclays Bank and its imposing local head office in Bank Plain still has a member of the Gurney family as a working Director. The Gurneys, Barclays, Buxtons and Hoares—all famous banking families who have intermarried—are to be found living in Norfolk.

It is hard to say which is the main industry in Norwich, there is so much variety. The cloth trade has gone, except for one silk mill. At the turn of the century, the mustard works of Messrs J. & J. Colman were the biggest employers of labour, but although the ramifications of this firm embrace a large variety of foods, they no longer enjoy that distinction which is now held by a factory making electric motors. There are more than 20 shoe factories, mainly making high-class ladies' shoes. There is one of the major chocolate factories in England, and there is the largest Christmas cracker factory in the world. But in spite of this, people have been known to visit Norwich frequently yet be unaware that it had any industries at all. Most of these factories have little, perhaps only a brass plate at the door, to say what they are, and most of them are in parts of the city not usually seen by the visitor. Trading estates near the city boundaries, but relatively unobtrusive, have drawn many industries from the centre releasing land for commercial and residential purposes.

Besides the large firms there are many small businesses run by craftsmen. They take some finding, but in many cases their work is known not only in Britain but abroad. Such crafts as book-binding, the making of stained-glass windows and the restoration of antique furniture, organ building and many more occupations give great satisfaction to those who have pride in doing a worthwhile job and also to the customer who appreciates good things. Craftsmen of this type never lack work and I think that Norwich will always produce or attract men like them, for it provides a congenial atmosphere and the right public to support them.

The present century has seen the city grow to the limits of its boundaries, absorbing Eaton, with its thatched church, and the almost deserted village of Earlham, which consisted of a small ancient church, a house which was formerly the Rectory, and Earlham Hall. Now, as we have said, it is the site of the University of East Anglia, the main buildings of which occupy a beautiful site in the Yare valley to the south of the Hall, and also a mass of temporary buildings, known as the University Village, near the church. The main blocks are original in conception, each of the residential blocks being several storeys high; each storey is smaller in area than the one below, resulting in a pyramid. Unfortunately the effect is vitiated by the fact that the buildings are usually seen from above, except by their residents, and the eye is attracted and held by the clutter on top. Projecting box-like erections, which may be water tanks or something highly necessary, could have been disguised to fit in with the style of the floors beneath. A tall chimney completes the ruin of what might have been a very effective design. As it is, one has to force oneself to look down at the better part of the composition.

Earlham Hall, built mainly in the seventeenth century, was the home of the Gurney family in the early years of the nineteenth century. Its story has been told in Percy Lubbock's book *Earlham*, but no better description of Earlham could be found than the following passage from George Borrow's *Lavengro* (1851):

'At some distance from the city, behind a range of hilly ground which rises towards the south-west, is a small river, the waters of which, after many meanderings, eventually enter the principal river of the district, and assist to swell the tide which rolls down to the ocean. It is a sweet rivulet, and pleasant it is to trace its course from spring-head, high up in the remote regions of Eastern Anglia, till it arrives in the valley behind yon rising ground; and pleasant is that valley, truly a good spot, but most lovely where yonder bridge crosses the little stream. Beneath its arch the waters rush garrulously into a blue pool, and are there stilled for a time, for the pool is deep, and they appear to have sunk to sleep. Farther on, however, you hear their voice again, where they ripple gaily over yon gravelly shallow. On the left the hill slopes gently down to the margin of the stream. On the right is a green level, a smiling meadow, grass of the richest decks the side of the slope; mighty trees also adorn it, giant elms, the nearest of which, when the sun is nigh its meridian, fling a broad shadow upon the face of the ancient brick of an old English Hall. It has a stately look, that old building, indistinctly seen, as it is, among those umbrageous trees.'

Very little has altered since Borrow wrote this passage. The old bridge has been replaced by a new one, and steps have been built to make it easier for children to paddle in the pool. Otherwise nothing is changed. The bridge which Borrow saw was built in 1744 and demolished in 1971. It was the second successor to one built of stone in 1502, by the will of Thomas Bachcroft of Little Melton, a parish some two miles farther from Norwich on this road. Bachcroft gave his estate to be sold for that purpose, 'and to make a stone cross by it, and put on it a scripture desiring the passengers to pray for his soul, and the souls of Margaret his wife, his father's and mother's, and of Thomas Northwold, and Margaret his wife'. The people who cross the new bridge are unlikely to pray for the members of Norfolk County Council who provided the present bridge.

Norwich is a city with a past to be proud of and a future in which it has every confidence. It cares very much for its past and preserves its old buildings, realizing that they are a great heritage and an asset. Mistakes may have been made from time to time, but changes are not entered into lightly. A comparison of Norwich today and as it was even a quarter of a century ago will show that the buildings are better cared for, and, if the paintings of the Norwich School which have come down to us from the early years of the nineteenth century are anything to go by, it is a wonder that this great heritage of buildings has survived at all—or did the painters prefer the dilapidated as being more romantic?

CHAPTER THREE

The Broads

Norwich is the gateway to the Norfolk Broads, that part of the county which is best known, at least by name, to the outsider. A well-known view of Norwich is of Pull's Ferry, an ancient water-gate which guarded the entrance to a canal which once enabled boats to pass from the River Wensum to within a few yards of the Cathedral so that, as we have seen, stone from Caen in Normandy could be delivered to the site when it, and the monastic buildings which surround it, were being built. The canal has long since been filled in, but in the summer many boats are moored near its entrance when their owners or hirers visit Norwich during a holiday on the Broads. From this point they enjoy a splendid view of the Cathedral across the Norwich School playing field, the spire, the second highest in England, showing to its best advantage from this low-lying view-point.

'What are Broads?' you may ask. They are about 200 miles of inter-communicating inland waterways, partly lakes, partly rivers, which lie in the area bounded by Norwich, Beccles, Lowestoft, Great Yarmouth and North Walsham. Until a few years ago, the origin of the lakes (broad water as opposed to the narrow river) was in doubt, but it has now been established that they are man-made. They are the result of extensive digging for peat in the Middle Ages, when, with the lack of coal supplies, peat was the chief fuel apart from wood. It is recorded in the account rolls of Norwich Cathedral Priory that in one year (1316) 400,000 peat turves were purchased. In course of time the pits from which the peat had been dug became flooded and channels were cut in order to connect them with the rivers.

Broadland was inhabited by independent men who lived by wild-fowling and fishing, and a number of them continued this manner of life until within living memory. They learned about the ways of birds and wild creatures in the course of their struggle for existence and much of their lore has been recorded, as well as anecdotes of their adventures. It is only about a hundred years since the Broads were first used for sailing for pleasure in the present-day sense. Previously, in addition to their use for wildfowling, they had proved useful for transport, as the staithes or landing places near the towns and villages testify, and sailing barges, called wherries, with large brown sails were used for transporting cargoes of produce to and from these places. Only one wherry, *Albion*, survives as the result of the efforts of a preservation society set up by enthusiasts, and it is kept in good operational condition. There has been a great increase in the use of the Broads for cruising since the introduction of motor cruisers which can be operated by people with no skill in sailing. Unfortunately this leads to novices with small knowledge of the rules of navigation being allowed to take charge of quite large boats. The peace and charm of the quiet waters is sometimes destroyed, but there are still some private Broads which remain undisturbed. The whole area can provide ideal conditions for sailing in calm waters unruffled except by the wash of passing boats. As many visitors only stop at recognized landing places, the wild life on the banks, both flora and fauna, continues to flourish. It is a paradise for naturalists. Many rare birds and insects breed here. Much has been written about them and much pleasure and knowledge has been gained by those who observe them.

The Broads are becoming smaller year by year: some of them have already become almost completely overgrown. Vegetation decays in the water and the natural process of forming fresh peat begins again, reducing the depth of the water so that more plants may grow until the accumulation of dead vegetable matter reaches the surface of the water and finally rises above it. Proposals have been made to reverse this process and develop areas, particularly in the southern part of the Broads, so as to provide a greater area of water for sailing.

Broadland can only be explored satisfactorily by boat. A lifetime of driving about in a car will reveal little. Roads cross rivers in places; they lead to staithes in others, often ending in a cul-de-sac, and between Acle and Yarmouth, where the country is open, the sails of craft can be seen from the road apparently gliding over the fields. But in general the Broads lie away from the roads or are obscured by trees and access is obstructed by private land or the gardens of houses which stand near the rivers.

As well as being a popular holiday resort, Broadland has developed into a residential area, for it lies within easy distance of three of the largest towns in East Anglia : Norwich, Great Yarmouth and Lowestoft. It is popular with people who commute daily to their work as well as being attractive to some who wish to retire, or to pursue occupations such as painting, writing or other artistic work in quiet rural surroundings. It is noticeable that a large proportion of people who work in Norwich prefer to live in the country rather than in the suburbs. In the Middle Ages and the Tudor period successful cloth merchants in Norwich married into county families and acquired country estates. The process has continued and the banking, professional and business families of the eighteenth, nineteenth and twentieth centuries have tended to live outside the city, often at a distance. They have very often combined farming and country pursuits with their business activities. Instead of residential suburbs linked with Norwich the Broadland villages such as Wroxham and Brundall have acquired the air of suburbs although separated by several miles from the towns. Thorpe St Andrew, which is now indistinguishable from Norwich, was an early Victorian riverside development at a time when it would not have been convenient to commute farther afield. Some of the large houses from that period still remain on the hillside overlooking that stretch of the river which looks so crowded and gay in J. Stannard's picture, 'Thorpe Water Frolic', painted in 1830. A large mid-Victorian church, built in 1866 to cater for the increased population, stands behind the ruins of the much smaller church through which one has to pass to reach its entrance. Though to the outsider Thorpe may appear to be part of Norwich, the inhabitants successfully resisted the combined efforts of Whitehall and Norwich to include it in the city boundaries, as also did the residents of Cringleford on the western fringe of Norwich.

The country in Broadland is not entirely flat as some people suppose. In many places steep banks rise from the rivers; for instance Belaugh Church stands boldly on an eminence close to the river, and below Norwich hills rise to the south of the River Yare and a ridge of high ground to the north separates it from the valley of the River Bure where many of the Broads are grouped. Higher ground to the south-east of Norwich causes the River Waveney to make a wide sweep before it joins the Yare at Breydon Water. But it is in the area west of Great Yarmouth, as far inland as Acle on the River Bure, that the country is really flat marshland intersected by ditches and virtually uninhabited. Derelict windmills once used for drainage are dotted about, and the sails of boats, riding upon water invisible to the eye, appear to be sailing over the fields. The scene recalls Holland. The River Yare is tidal to the centre of Norwich, and sea-going vessels bring cargoes to the city. Much of the Broads area is tidal and many a novice has woken up to find he has moored on a mudbank and has to wait for the next tide before he can either move his boat or go ashore. If he has moored against a bank he may well discover that he and his family are rolling out of their bunks as the boat heels over with the receding tide. The amateur who knows scarcely anything about navigation or the rules of sailing and who drives a motor cruiser as he would a car, forgetting that there are no brakes, can be dangerous.

Broadland villages are probably more sophisticated than those in the rest of Norfolk. Their shops must cater not only for the needs of the inhabitants but for those of the holidaymaker as well. At Wroxham for many years the enterprise of one firm has resulted in its becoming 'universal providers' and spreading over most of the village centre, claiming to be 'the largest village store in the world'. This firm provides the street lighting, public lavatories and car parking, and with traffic congestion in Norwich it now sets out to attract shoppers from the city seven miles away.

The villages of Wroxham and Hoveton have merged into one and together form the largest centre actually in Broadland. Wroxham Church has a very fine Norman doorway which has somehow turned blue! Hoveton Church stands about a mile away on the road to Horning where hotels, shops and boathouses line the village street which runs along the north bank of the River Bure. Private houses, many of them with boathouses or little docks of their own, continue for about a mile. The road from Horning to Ludham crosses the River Ant. Ludham is a pleasant village, as is its neighbour Catfield which lies some two or three miles to the north, but although they are Broadland villages they do not stand on the banks of either rivers or Broads, as Wroxham and Horning do, but are each about a mile from the water. Stalham, which is a busy village with a number of shops, can be approached by water from Sutton Broad.

Farther west, beyond Wroxham, Coltishall and Horstead, two straggling villages which are merging together, provide one of the more popular mooring places on the River Bure.

As a favoured residential area there is, at best, a self-conscious 'grooming' about some of the countryside and it is not surprising that Woodbastwick has won a prize as being the best-kept Norfolk village. Ranworth, nearby, is a great attraction as the view of the countryside from the tower of its fine church is a rare opportunity to see Broadland other than at close quarters. The light, airy church with its wide nave is worth seeing for its remarkable early fifteenth-century screen with two projecting wings which each housed an altar. The paintings of the 12 apostles are particularly well preserved. There is also an ancient wooden lectern. The famous *Ranworth Antiphoner*, a large illuminated book of the Psalms with plainsong accompaniment, probably written and illuminated by the monks of Langley Abbey in about 1400 and used at Ranworth Church until 1552 when it was ordered to be destroyed, was discovered in 1912 in a London bookshop and was re-purchased for the Parish of Ranworth. It is now in the safe-keeping of Norwich Castle Museum.

Several other Broadland churches besides Ranworth have well preserved painted screens, a number of them featuring East Anglian saints. There are also the remains of many wall paintings. Some of the churches are large and as in most cases in Norfolk, seldom lack interest. At South Walsham, not far from Ranworth, two churches stand in the same churchyard, but this is by no means uncommon in the county. In this case each church had its own parish. St Lawrence was burnt down in 1827, but though the chancel was restored and re-opened in 1832, the nave is gone and half the tower stands, split from top to bottom, as it has done ever since the fire. It looks most unsafe, but for 150 years it has belied its appearance. Another instance of two churches standing in the same churchyard is at Great Melton some six or seven miles to the west of Norwich. Here there were All Saints and St Mary's. Apparently All Saints became dilapidated long ago; it was in that state in the time of Queen Anne, but in 1883 it was rebuilt and St Mary's was allowed to fall into ruin so that today nothing but the tower remains. A somewhat similar state of affairs exists at Gillingham, near Beccles, which is mentioned elsewhere, and there are other instances in the county.

A few miles south-east of South Walsham is the little market town of Acle, where a bridge crosses the River Bure providing the only link by road between the two parts of the northern half of Broadland. The link between the northern broads and those of the southern area, the Rivers Yare and Waveney and the Broads connected with them, is at Great Yarmouth, where all the rivers of the system flow into the sea through one common mouth. At Acle the country changes. The upper reaches of the Bure pass through undulating country which is well wooded, but from Acle to the sea the country is flat and marshy and the river has been embanked to prevent it flooding the surrounding land. The pasture land is intersected by ditches and the remains of disused windmills, formerly used to lift water from the ditches into the higher waters of the river, are dotted about, giving relief to the monotony.

Two roads lead from Acle to Yarmouth. The old road skirting the northern edge of the marsh through the villages of Billockby and Filby, and Acle New Road which lies south of the river and runs straight as a die in two stretches of two and a half and five miles respectively. It carries the bulk of the considerable traffic. The skyline of Great Yarmouth lies straight ahead, and the wind can sweep across the road except for the ineffectual hindrance of a line of pollarded willow trees on the south side. It is not a road to tempt anyone to dawdle and no one does.

There are at least ten villages, on or near the old road, with names ending in -by, a sign that they were originally Danish settlements. It

14 *Ranworth Broad from the church tower*

is a more pleasant route than the New Road, with one of the few opportunities to see one of the larger broads where the road crosses Filby Broad, giving views of wide stretches of water on either side.

The Broads to the north are linked by the River Thurne, which rises a few yards from the sea north of Winterton and flows directly away from it to join the Bure some miles inland. The River Ant, which joins the Bure some two or three miles farther upstream from Acle, rises in the North Walsham area and, like the Thurne, seems to make no attempt to reach the sea. Both the Thurne and the Ant flow through flat country which is more open than the upper reaches of the Bure and the Yare. Potter Heigham is the most popular centre for this area and the holidaymaker is well catered for by the big shops and other facilities near the bridge. Potter Heigham Bridge is a trap for the unwary as the opening is small; boats frequently find insufficient headroom and get stuck. The part of Potter Heigham which the visitor sees is by no means attractive. The real village a mile away is probably not seen by the majority, and the same is true of Ludham, where the river is the best part of two miles from the pleasant village with its large and interesting church with a good painted screen, and some attractive old houses. The majority of the villages in Broadland are not close to the rivers, and it is evident that when the settlements were founded it was not thought necessary to place them near a river.

South of Ludham, and inaccessible except by water, is St Benet's Abbey, a ruin with a tower of a windmill incorporated in the scanty remains of a once wealthy and important Abbey. By some oversight the Bishop of Norwich remained Abbot of St Benet's at the Holme after the Dissolution of the Monasteries and until recent times sat in the House of Lords as the only surviving mitred abbot. The Bishop of Norwich goes by boat once a year and conducts an open-air service amid the ruins.

Hickling and Barton Broads are lakes covering a considerable area, but the largest area of water is Breydon Water, the tidal land-locked estuary of the Rivers Yare and Waveney. The coastline at Great Yarmouth has undergone considerable changes in historic times and so has Breydon Water, but at the actual confluence of the two rivers the bank is as it has been for 1,700 years, for here stands the massive and impressive Burgh Castle, an oblong area of six acres enclosed by a massive wall 9 feet thick and about 20 feet high with solid bastions at intervals. Most of this great wall remains intact. The scene is little different from what it was when, as Roman Gariannonum, it was one of the forts of the Saxon Shore which extended from the Wash round the east and south coast of England to Porchester, to defend Britain from Saxon invaders. But these defences were of no avail once the Romans had withdrawn and left the inhabitants of Britain to their fate and a great civilization vanished.

Both the Yare and the Waveney meander through many twists and turns. Suggestions have been made to develop the latter so as to relieve the pressure on the northern part of Broadland. The little River Chet, a tributary of the Waveney, is navigable as far as Loddon, where a boat yard re-opened a few years ago. Oulton Broad leads into the heart of Lowestoft and here there is a considerable shipbuilding industry besides the fishing fleet. The Waveney flows through Beccles, which is one of the starting places for holidays on the Broads.

Although not strictly part of Broadland, the towns of Aylsham and North Walsham lie on its northern borders and have some connections with it, for the River Bure passes through Aylsham and at one time there was traffic by river to and from a dock on the Banningham Road. North Walsham used to be connected with Barton Broad by the North Walsham & Dilham Canal so that the town could benefit from water transport, but the canal has been derelict for many years, though there are plans to restore it for pleasure traffic. Part of the canal can be seen where it is crossed by the road to Mundesley. North Walsham is the market town for Mundesley, Bacton and Happisburgh and the northern part of the Broads. It is the centre of the Norfolk reed thatching industry and skilled thatchers with lorries piled high with bundles of reeds often travel for hundreds of miles to thatch houses. Norfolk reed is the most durable material for this purpose and much of it is grown at Horsey and elsewhere. Norfolk thatching is not so decorative as, say, the straw thatching of Wiltshire, but it lasts a great deal longer. The reeds also used to be laid under the tiles of houses in East Anglia as a form of insulation. There are still many houses with thatched roofs in Norfolk and a number of churches as well, and in the centre of Norwich two buildings known as the Briton's Arms, now a restaurant, and the Barking Dickey, which is a bank, are both thatched. After a great fire which took place in 1507 when 718 houses were destroyed, no more thatched houses were allowed to be built in the city.

North Walsham Church is big and has a partially ruined tower which fell in 1724. There is an interesting Market Cross built of timber, with a lead-covered domed roof and lantern, which dates from 1602. The Paston Grammar School, which Nelson attended for three years, has a building dating from 1765. The road from North Walsham to Norwich passes through Westwick Park, with a pretty stretch lined with rhododendrons near a lake, and soon afterwards through Westwick Arch, formerly the entrance to the estate; the arch is built of flint with brick dressings. Here a turning leads to Worstead, once the town which gave its name to the woollen cloth. The great 'wool' church dominates the village which is all that is left of the old town, bearing witness to the wealth of its merchants in the latter part of the fourteenth century. The building of the church began in 1379 and was finished about 1400. It is about 130 feet long and the tower is 109 feet high. The chancel may be a little earlier than the rest of the building. The stonework of the exterior is highly decorated but the interior is plainer. As in some other large Norfolk churches, for instance Cley, Walpole St Peter and Salle, there has been no attempt to fill the building with seats and the aisles and the western part of the nave present an uncluttered spacious appearance. The two blocks of box pews in the nave are neat and practical as a protection from draughts. The west side of them is of high panelling with fluted pilasters at the corners. Not content with a fine rood screen dated 1512, which is unusually high, though suitable for the large chancel arch, and the parclose screens which form its continuation across the north and south aisles, there is another fine screen across the tower arch bearing the date 1501, though its excellent condition might first give the impression that it is modern. The fact that the style of the figures in the painted panels are so unlike anything medieval also causes doubt. However, they were painted in 1831 and are copies of the windows in the Chapel of New College,

Oxford, designed by Sir Joshua Reynolds. In front of it stands the font with a pretty Perpendicular cover. A hammerbeam roof covers the nave. During the past few years large sums of money have been spent on restoration and have been raised largely through local enterprise. Some of it has been contributed by businesses connected with the manufacture and use of cloth: a happy thought on someone's part. Outside the church many of the houses are survivals from the great days of Worstead.

Aylsham lies midway between Norwich and Cromer, but the through traffic by-passes the Market Place, which is considerable for the size of the town and retains its original character. The large church on its north side is interesting. It is associated with the Reptons, father and son, who have been mentioned elsewhere as the designers of, among other places, Sheringham Hall and its park. The grave of Humphrey Repton outside the south side of the church has been restored by admirers. Repton, when called upon to improve an estate, would draw a picture of it as it was and superimpose cut-out flaps painted to show what the result would be after he had planted trees and made other alterations to the landscape. These have been preserved in a number of cases. His epitaph, composed by himself, reads:

> *Not like Egyptian tyrants consecrate,*
> *Unmixed with others shall my dust remain;*
> *But mold'ring, blending, melting into earth*
> *Mine shall give form and colour to the Rose,*
> *And while its vivid blossoms cheer Mankind,*
> *Its perfumed odours shall ascend to Heaven.*

The restorers of the monument have planted fresh rose bushes on the grave.

There are a number of pleasant eighteenth-century brick buildings in the town and two nice houses of about 1700 on the road to Blickling, which is about one-and-a-half miles to the west; here at a dip in the road just past the church, there is a surprise view of the front of Blickling Hall dramatically set back from the road at the end of a drive between wide lawns, the width of the house, flanked by massive yew hedges which cause one to wonder how they can possibly be trimmed so evenly. The hedges' lines are continued by ranges of seventeenth-century domestic buildings and the front of the house bears the date 1620. It is built of red brick with stone dressings and presents an exciting skyline of corner turrets, Dutch gables and Tudor style chimneys. The architect, Robert Liminge or Lyminge, also designed Hatfield House, but in the eighteenth century additions and alterations were made very sympathetically by Thomas and William Ivory, the Norwich architects. It was Thomas Ivory who remodelled the entrance hall, using the old staircase, which had been placed unobtrusively to one side, as the basis for the present grand staircase in the centre of the building. Life-size reliefs, carved in wood, of Anne Boleyn and Queen Elizabeth I, her daughter, which stand in niches above the stairs, remind us that Blickling was the childhood home of Anne, though it is not certain that she was born in the house which stood on this site before the present one was built.

The most impressive room in the house is the library, which is 127 feet long and has a most elaborate moulded plaster ceiling with panels depicting, among other things, the Five Senses and Learning. The ceiling was constructed between 1620-30. The windows of this long room look out upon the beautiful formal garden, with flower beds round a fountain brought from Oxnead Hall, the former home of the Pastons, and large clumps of yew trimmed into shapes curiously resembling grand pianos. Beyond the formal garden, a wide vista stretches up a slope towards a summer house in the form of a Tuscan temple. From the temple vistas through the trees can be seen in different directions. There is also a park with a lake which invites exploration.

Blickling has a history long preceding the present house. Its famous owners are said to include King Harold. Herbert de Losinga, the first Bishop of Norwich, owned it, later it came into the possession of Sir Thomas Erpingham, and later still of Sir John Fastolf who built Caister Castle. It then passed to Geoffrey Boleyn, grandfather of Anne. The next owner was Sir Henry Hobart, who had a house in Norwich on the site of the present Assembly House and it was by him that the present Blickling Hall was built. The Hobarts became Earls of Buckingham and through them the estate came to the Marquis of Lothian. The 11th Marquis, who was at one time British Ambassador to the United States of America, left the estate to the National Trust. His tomb, and that of the 8th Marquis (designed by G. F. Watts), and many memorials to previous inhabitants of the Hall are to be seen in the very greatly restored parish church. There are many memorial brasses in the church, including several to members of the Boleyn family, but the finest is that to Sir Nicholas Dagworth, dated 1401.

The fate of Anne Boleyn, who was beheaded by order of her husband Henry VIII, has led to a number of ghost stories and her connection with Blickling has inevitably produced one of them. On the anniversary of her execution she is said to ride up to the Hall in a coach drawn by headless horses driven by a headless coachman, while Anne sits with her head on her lap. Her father's ghost too, is said to have to cross 40 bridges in one night in a similar coach.

The River Bure flows to the north of Blickling Park between it and the park of Wolterton Hall, built by Thomas Ripley between 1727 and 1741 for Horatio Walpole and now occupied by the present Lord Walpole. Ripley had worked for Sir Robert Walpole at Houghton from 1722 and although the exteriors of the two houses bear no resemblance to each other there are similarities inside. The exterior of Wolterton is of red brick with a Portland stone lower storey on the garden side which looks over a lake. As at Houghton, the exterior flight of stairs, which once gave access to the Marble Hall on the first floor which connected with the state rooms, has been lost and the entrance on the ground floor leads into a low-pitched hall. A bust of Lord Nelson in this entrance hall reminds us that he was named Horatio after his cousin the second Lord Walpole. About 1830 a wing was added to the east of the building by George Stanley Repton who also added the stone arcade and steps on the south front of the house.

Another fine house is Barningham Hall about three miles to the north of Wolterton. There are three Barninghams; the Hall to which I refer is at Town Barningham, sometimes called Winter Barningham in reference to the family of that name which lived here in the Middle Ages before the present house was built for Sir Edward Paston in 1612. The Hall stands in a beautiful park overlooking a lake which is one of the sources of the River Bure. The Hall is built of brick with stone dressings and presents a mass of mullioned and transomed windows crowned with stepped gables and pinnacles. The effect of height is enhanced by the two-storey dormer windows. The house was enlarged by J. A. Repton in 1805 without affecting the appearance of the front.

Close to Wolterton, spanning the main stream of the River Bure, is Itteringham Mill, now a guest house and a popular resort for afternoon teas—a facility rare in Norfolk.

South of Norwich the country lying to the east of the Norwich-to-Beccles road borders the southern part of the Broads. One leaves Norwich by Trowse Bridge, over which much of the food which Norwich consumes is said to come into the city. This is another way of saying that the country in this direction is good market gardening land, a fact borne out by the names of the tenants of the stalls on Norwich Market Place, many of whom come from Kirby Bedon, Bergh Apton, Surlingham, Hellington and other villages in the neighbourhood. A long, steep hill rises to Crown Point where the house was formerly the home of the Colman family whose name became synonymous with mustard. At the turn of the century they were the largest employers of labour in Norwich. Between the Norwich to Beccles road and the rivers Yare and Waveney, there is a network of lanes which serve the villages and the marshes, but carry no through traffic, thus leaving these places quiet and unspoiled. It is true that there is the A.143 which leads to Yarmouth, cutting off a bend in the river, but it does not affect most of the area.

Langley Park estate lies to the north of Loddon, the mansion now being a school. Its fine rooms with elaborate plaster-work remain. The house was designed by Matthew Brettingham, who was responsible for building Holkham Hall under William Kent in the 1740s. Another mansion to the south-east of Loddon is Raveningham Hall, the seat of Sir Edmund Bacon, Bart, the premier Baronet of England, who is also Lord Lieutenant of Norfolk. The exterior of the house is not exciting but it contains a fine collection of pictures, including drawings of the Norwich School and some Constable cloud studies.

Loddon has some Georgian houses and a fifteenth-century church.

The District Council which serves the area has been responsible for some very good council houses designed by the architects Tayler and Green. Groups of these attractive houses are to be found not only at Loddon, but at Hales, Thurton, Bergh Apton, Gillingham and elsewhere. They show how even today architecture can enhance its surroundings.

The churches of the country bordering the southern Broads are mainly small Norman buildings; several are thatched and have round towers and fine Norman doorways. The proximity of the river lends colour to the theory that the round towers were originally built for defence against raiding Norsemen who could sail up these rivers with ease. After centuries of peace there is again a threat of a different sort of invasion from this quarter, this time an unarmed one by holidaymakers in motor cruisers, for there is talk of developing the River Waveney to relieve the pressure on the northern part of Broadland.

The most interesting of the Norman churches is at Hales. It stands alone in a field some distance from the village and is perhaps the best example of an unspoiled Norman church we are likely to find. It has a round tower with the marks of the wicker-work forms used by the Saxon workmen to make the round double-splay windows; there is a thatched roof and a round apse with blind arcading on the outside. As with other churches in the neighbourhood it has a fine Norman doorway. Heckingham Church has features similar to Hales, and may well have been built by the same craftsmen, and other churches in the neighbourhood are well worth a visit. Toft Monks has an octagonal tower: not just the top storey, as in so many instances, but octagonal from the ground upwards; there is a very modern east window.

At Buckenham a few miles to the North, on the opposite bank of the River Yare, there is a similar octagonal tower to the one at Toft Monks. Burgh St Peter has a curious brick tower built in a series of square storeys each smaller than the one below, and Haddiscoe Church has some interesting features.

Between Hales and Beccles is Gillingham Hall, a red-brick Jacobean house lying back from the road and almost marooned by road improvements. In its grounds near the road are three churches; only the tower of All Saints remains; the rest fell in 1748. St Mary's is a Norman church which was over-restored in the middle of the nineteenth century and looks unusual as a result. A short distance from these two buildings is a Roman Catholic church—the Todhunter family, to whom the Hall belongs, are Roman Catholics—a red-brick building of 1898, in an Italian style with two west towers.

From Gillingham we look across the marshes and the River Waveney towards the picturesque skyline of Beccles. The large parish church there has a massive detached tower and to the right rises the tower of the Roman Catholic church which was built in 1889 in an excellent imitation of the French Romanesque style. The corner stair turret which rises above the tower gives a somewhat castle-like effect when seen from this distance.

Beccles is the southern limit of the Broads and is one of the boat-hiring centres. It is a pleasant market town with some interesting buildings, but being in Suffolk is outside my terms of reference. So too is Bungay some seven miles to the west, higher up the River Waveney, which is frequently in flood along much of its course above Beccles. There are the massive remains of a castle at Bungay, which was built by Roger Bigod who also built Norwich Castle. Both Beccles and Bungay, like Norwich and Fakenham, have large printing works mainly engaged in producing books. On the Norfolk side of the river facing Bungay is Ditchingham, a pretty place with several features of interest mentioned in another chapter.

The Waveney valley continues through Harleston, but we will set out again from Norwich and explore a different route by way of the valley of the little River Tas, in another chapter.

CHAPTER FOUR

The Coast

If Norfolk is an important agricultural county, it has also a long coastline, extending for nearly a hundred miles, and as a result the sea has always exerted a strong influence. The livelihood of many depends upon the sea, directly or indirectly, even today. Well into the twentieth century many farm workers went to sea as soon as the harvest was gathered in and worked in fishing boats throughout the herring season and the winter until spring brought more work on the land. Now it is the holiday industry which creates work along the coast. Since the discovery of natural gas in the North Sea a new industry has sprung into being, of ferrying supplies to the oil rigs and this includes catering for the oil-rig crews.

The East Coast may have been one of the points where successive waves of immigrants landed in Britain in pre-historic times: it certainly was the point of their arrival during historic times. The problem of invasion exercised the minds of the Romans who built the series of fortresses which were under the jurisdiction of the Count of the Saxon Shore. They extended from the Wash southwards as far as Porchester in Hampshire and two of them, Brancaster and Burgh Castle defended Norfolk. There was also a signal station at Thornham; another at Corton near Lowestoft, and probably another on a hilltop near Stiffkey, and possibly others, all traces of which have disappeared. When the Romans departed, the invasion by Angles and Saxons found no resistance and later, particularly between the years 841 and 1069, the region was invaded by the Danes. The Angles gave their name to the Kingdom of East Anglia and ultimately to England. Like their predecessors they tended to settle in the coastal areas of Norfolk, both in the East and the West of the county, and in those days when the Fens were mostly under water the western area included the higher ground bordering the Fens in the Downham Market neighbourhood. Mid-Norfolk was largely covered by forest which the Romans had started to clear and the Angles and Saxons continued the process. It was up the rivers that the Danes sailed in their shallow-draught boats, leaving evidence of their settlements in place names.

When peace came after the Norman Conquest trade developed. Great Yarmouth and King's Lynn developed considerable trade with the Continent and small ports between them did coastal trading or sent small ships to Holland and elsewhere. The increase in size of ships in the nineteenth century led to the decline of these ports, but King's Lynn is reviving. The invasions which have come to Norfolk during the centuries since the Norman Conquest have been peaceful. The Flemings, introduced in the Middle Ages, brought their skills in weaving, and the Huguenots and Dutch in the sixteenth century. No armed invasions have taken place on the Norfolk coast since the time of the Danes, but one wonders whether there was any truth in the suggestion in Erskine Childers' book, *The Riddle of the Sands*, that Germany was planning an invasion via the Wash by barges from the area round the mouth of the Elbe, before 1914. Throughout the centuries there has always been a fear that invasion might take place somewhere along the Norfolk coast owing to the fact that at Weybourne there is deep water near the cliffs so that large ships may anchor near to the shore. An old rhyme says:

> *He who would old England win*
> *Must at Weybourne Hoop begin.*

Besides Great Yarmouth and King's Lynn, Norwich and Wells-next-the-Sea handle a small amount of shipping, but the remaining navigable channels at Blakeney, Brancaster and Burnham Overy only provide for small yachts and dinghys.

The coast is dangerous, with a consequent toll of life in the storms which beat upon it from the North Sea, and the churches of coastal villages such as Winterton and Sea Palling, contain boards on which are recorded the rescues made by the local lifeboats and the many lives lost. On one occasion in 1662, 200 small colliers were sailing northwards from Yarmouth when a gale sprang up near Winterton Ness and 140 of them were dashed to pieces, with scarcely a soul saved. The same night another fleet of little ships, sailing in the opposite direction, was caught in the storm and brought the total number wrecked to 200 and the lives lost to 1,000. Shelter can be found for ships in Yarmouth Roads, a channel running parallel with the coast, which is protected by a sandbank from the full force of the waves. This bank, known as Scroby Sands, is a home for a large colony of seals which are attractive to visitors. There are other colonies of seals on sandbanks in the Wash.

With improvements in lifeboats fewer need be stationed around this coast, for modern boats can operate over longer distances; but the number of calls for help remains high. The former coxswain of the Cromer lifeboat Henry Blogg, has become a local hero and his name is commemorated at Cromer, where he served for many years; a bronze bust of his weather-beaten face looks out to sea.

The map of Norfolk shows a smooth coastline stretching north-wards from Great Yarmouth, like a quarter segment of a circle with its centre at Norwich. At Weybourne it turns due west for about 25 miles and consists mainly of salt marshes intersected by innumer-able creeks; then, at Hunstanton, the coast abruptly turns south to form the east side of the Wash, along the southern side of which it runs westwards till it meets the coast of Lincolnshire. It is the smooth, unbroken coast, consisting of fine sands flanked by dunes, which form the only protection for the low-lying land behind, and it is this coast which is so dangerous to shipping. The sea here should be treated with respect by the swimmer, for there are strong cur-rents. It is a lonely coast and even the visitors who stay in caravans behind the sand dunes and those who come for the day cannot crowd the wide sands. Winterton claims to be the driest spot in the British Isles and there is much sunshine and bracing wind. The sea has been known to break through the slender defences: twice in the century much of the land in the Horsey and Sea Palling area has been flooded, and yet a glance at the villages and their churches shows that for centuries Norfolk people have lived here. Marram grass, which binds the sand together, has been planted on the dunes to prevent erosion by wind and water. At Happisburgh, the land begins to rise gently and continues to do so until at Trimingham the cliffs are over 200 feet high, but another problem is then found, for the cliffs here and at Overstrand are fast falling into the sea. Underground springs of water flow from the face of the cliff and cause landslides, the debris from which is soon carried southwards along the coast by the current.

The land in north-east Norfolk is fertile and bears witness to its prosperity in the past by the large number of churches, all of interest and many exceptionally fine. Viewed from Happisburgh or Trimingham the church towers seem innumerable. Happisburgh Church itself has a tower of 110 feet high and, with the nearby lighthouse, forms a conspicuous landmark. But we are going too fast and leaving the second largest town in Norfolk behind.

Great Yarmouth is a curious mixture. There is the old town, once an important seaport and until recently one of the great fishing ports of the country, and there is the holiday resort which thrives on trippers and, in a way, seems so unlike Norfolk. But it is Norfolk on holiday, as well as the resort of thousands from the Midlands and elsewhere. Suggestions have been made for linking Great Yarmouth and Lowestoft to form one large city—in spite of the fact that Lowestoft is in Suffolk. There is something to be said for this, for although the River Waveney forms the boundary between the counties, it turns north for several miles before joining the River Yare at Yarmouth, then doubles back southwards for some three miles in order to reach the sea. The result is the Lothingland Peninsula—part of Suffolk projecting northwards along what might be the Norfolk coast. Gorleston, the southern suburb of Great Yarmouth, is already included in Norfolk, although on the Suffolk side of the river, and the whole Peninsula is in the diocese of Norwich, for ecclesiastical boundaries are more sensible than civil ones in many cases, as will be found in west Norfolk. It will therefore not seem to be an intrusion to say a few words about Lowestoft in a book about Norfolk.

Lowestoft is the most easterly point of the British Isles and draws attention to this fact by depicting the rising sun in its coat of arms. Like Yarmouth it combines industry with the amenities of a seaside resort, though it tends to place less emphasis on the holiday industry. The fishing fleet, with its fine docks, used to be the most important industry, but, like Yarmouth, this has suffered what it is to be hoped is a temporary set-back owing to the poor catches of herring for a number of years. However, there is a flourishing shipbuilding industry and a high proportion of all the motor buses in Great Britain are built here. There are a number of other factories, so it is not a seaside resort which closes down and becomes deserted out of season. There is a fine church to show that the town has ancient origins, but most of the development is Victorian.

The coast between Lowestoft and Yarmouth is edged with holiday camps. Inland is the village of Blundeston made famous by Dickens as the scene of the birth of David Copperfield. The road from Blundeston to Yarmouth has changed very much since Barkis drove his carrier's cart to Yarmouth, and it is no use looking for the site of Peggoty's home in an upturned boat on the South Denes (though it is perhaps surprising that someone has not erected an authentic copy and commercialized it). However, a tablet on the Royal Hotel, Yarmouth, commemorates the fact that Charles Dickens stayed there.

It is difficult to suggest the best time to explore Yarmouth; in the summer the streets are crowded; in the winter they are bleak and the sea front deserted. However, there are a number of interesting features of the old town which deserve to be seen.

The land on which Yarmouth is built had risen from the sea in historic times. A map of the site as it was during the Roman occupation would show an entirely different coastline and the mouths of the River Yare and the River Waveney were a different shape. The shingle spit upon which the town stands has been deposited since then and is still growing eastward, as may be seen by the wide stretch of sand which is seldom washed by the sea and upon which a series of buildings for entertainment have been laid out: gardens, a swimming pool and amusement park and so on. However, the sandbank was large enough by the early Middle Ages for the town to have become firmly established as a thriving port and the town walls were begun in 1260 to form a semicircle on the eastern side, with its chord formed by the Quay which runs along the left bank of the river. Sections of the wall and some of the bastions remain.

The prefix 'Great' was conferred upon the town by Henry III in a charter dated 1272. The town looked westward towards the river, and not towards the sea, until the eighteenth century when it became fashionable to visit the seaside for pleasure. Great Yarmouth was quick to profit by the new fashion; consequently the development of the east side of the town which faces the sea dates mainly from the early years of the nineteenth century. The remainder of the town has either earlier or more modern buildings. Examples of old merchants' houses still survive near the South Quay and some of them are open to the public. There is a large Market Place, and the main streets run north and south, with the famous Rows connecting them from east to west. The Rows were originally 145 numbered passages, some not more than four feet wide, with houses on both sides facing each other. The Rows appear to date from the sixteenth century and they survived until the bombing during the Second World War destroyed a great many of them. Sufficient remain to give some indication of their former appearance. The sites of the Rows which have been destroyed have been used for modern flats and houses. It is said that when the high-water mark of the sea on the eastern side of the town was nearer its centre than it is today, the water would run through the Rows into the river beyond when there was a storm. Transport through the Rows was by means of a special type of cart resembling a wheelbarrow with either one or two wheels at the end opposite the shafts. One of these carts may be seen in the Bridewell Museum, Norwich, and another appears in a picture of Yarmouth Quay painted in 1823 by G. Vincent. This picture also shows a grove of trees growing on the Quay between the forest of masts and sails and the fronts of the houses.

St Nicholas Church has the largest floor area of any parish church in England. It suffered severely from bombing and stood for years a roofless ruin until it was rebuilt between 1957-60. The building dates mainly from the thirteenth century, although there is some Norman work at the base of the tower. The narrow nave preserves the original Norman plan, but the aisles are evidence of the increasing wealth of the town in the thirteenth century, which resulted in the building being exceptionally wide. The present arrangement of the interior is more like that of a cathedral than a parish church. There are pulpits and organ consoles in both the nave and the choir. The church is full of colour and, as during the rebuilding the opportunity was taken to remove alternate piers in the nave, there is greater visibility and light than formerly. The very fine modern iron screen-work was made by Mr E. A. Stevenson, the village blacksmith of Wroxham, who also made the gates of St Saviour's Chapel at Norwich Cathedral. For the work which he did for St Nicholas, Great Yarmouth, he was made a member of the Worshipful Company of Blacksmiths and a Freeman of the City of London, and at the same time he was given the Gold Medal of the Worshipful Company, the only one ever awarded by them to 'A Superlative Craftsman'. There is also some colourful modern stained glass in the east windows of the chancel and the south aisle.

Adjoining the churchyard is a nice Georgian vicarage built in 1718 and altered in 1781. Next door to it is a small timber-framed house which was the birthplace of Anna Sewell, the author of *Black Beauty*. Next to Sewell House and, like it and the Vicarage, facing Church Plain (notice how, as at Norwich, small open spaces and wide parts of roads are called Plains) is the Fishermen's Hospital, an attractive group of almshouses built by Yarmouth Corporation in 1702. Both the busy Hall Quay not far from the opposite end of the large Market Place, and its continuation, South Quay, have some interesting buildings. Number 4 South Quay, part of a medieval building with late sixteenth-century panelled rooms, is open to the public. It belongs to the National Trust. Outside, ships may be seen loading and unloading.

The northern and southern extremities of the town are known as the North Denes and South Denes respectively ('dene' means 'a bare sandy tract by the sea'). In the days of the herring fishery the South Denes were devoted to that industry. Buildings were mainly used for curing the famous Yarmouth bloaters; piles of logs were to be seen stacked against their walls to be burned in due course to provide the smoke for curing. The open spaces near the quay were used for cleaning the fish, by the large numbers of Scottish fishwives who came south for the season, and the remainder of the area was useful for drying nets and for storing the thousands of barrels in which the

16   *Great Yarmouth: Fishermen's Hospital founded 1702*
17   *Great Yarmouth: Georgian Houses, South Quay*

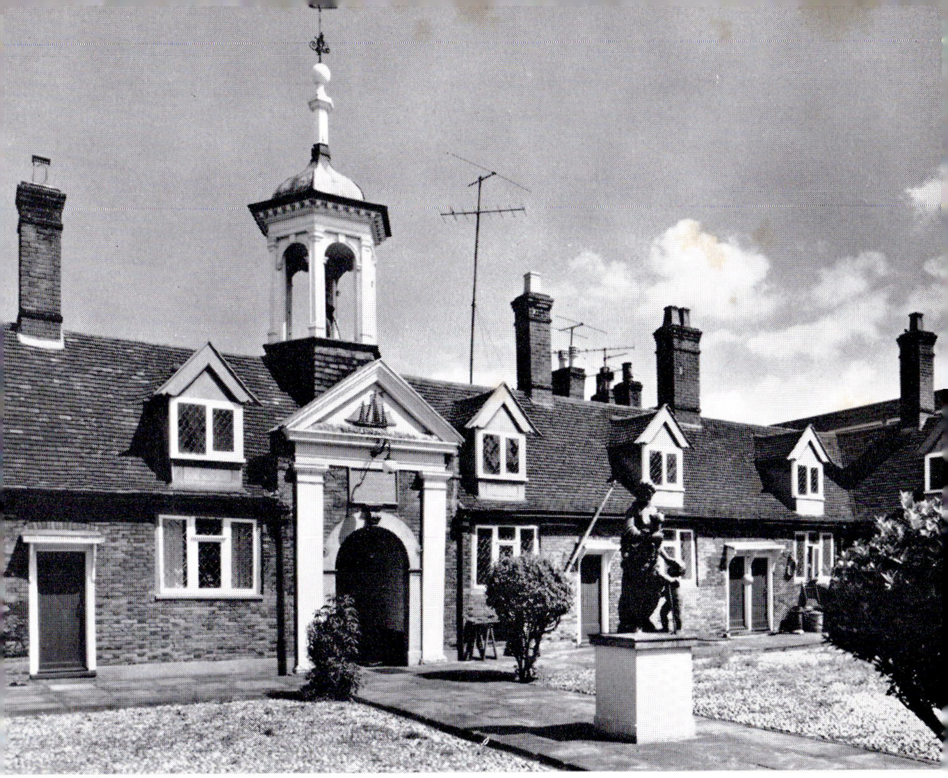

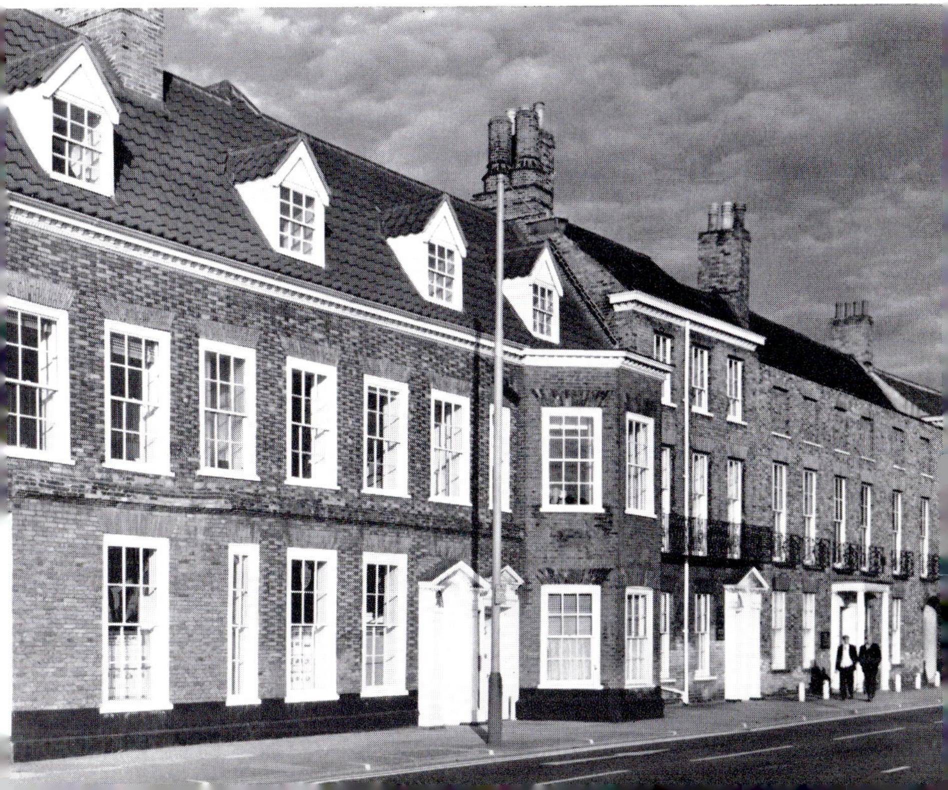

fish were packed. Now the western side of this part of the South Denes is devoted to a variety of industries and to a power station, while the seaward side has become a caravan park. In the middle of the South Denes stands the Nelson Column, erected to the memory of Norfolk's hero in 1817. It is only one foot shorter than the more famous column in Trafalgar Square and is surmounted by a figure of Britannia.

The amusements of Great Yarmouth cater for one public, but the long stretch of coastline which starts north of Caister-on-Sea caters for those who enjoy the sea and sands and can manage without the theatres and funfairs.

Caister-on-Sea is virtually a suburb of Yarmouth. Originally a Roman settlement, as its name implies, some of the excavated foundations of the Roman buildings may be seen. They include what is believed to be a seamen's boarding house. When built, this town stood at the mouth of an estuary which has been silted up. A short distance inland is Caister Castle, built, as we have seen, for Sir John Fastolf in 1432-5. There is a massive brick tower 98 feet high, and part of the walls, all standing within a moat. The Paston family, famous for their letters which have been preserved and form a valuable source of social history for the period, lived here from 1459 till 1599.

Beyond Caister there are a number of bungalows and holiday camps close to Ormesby and Hemsby, but north of Winterton the coast consists of wide bare sands flanked by sandhills crossed at intervals by concrete ramps constructed to prevent erosion by wind and traffic of this only defence against the sea. The hinterland between Winterton and Happisburgh is sparsely populated and Hickling Broad, Horsey Mere and Martham Broad lie in this area. Hickling Broad is the largest sheet of water in the Broads apart from the estuary of Breydon Water.

At Happisburgh the coast changes, rising so that low cliffs are formed behind narrower sands. Here the hinterland consists of fertile soil with evidence of cultivation and habitation over a long period. The land gradually rises until at Mundesley the cliffs reach 100 feet above sea level and at Trimingham over 220 feet. Cliffs continue along the coast until the salt marshes are reached at Salthouse

18 Cromer Church from the High Street

near Cley. Along this stretch of coast holiday resorts developed with the coming of the railways in the nineteenth century and some of the grandiose hotels of the 1897 Diamond Jubilee period still survive, though in some cases converted into flats. They form a memorial to a very different civilization from that represented by the caravans and beach huts which are to be found in groups between the seaside resorts.

Bacton has been a popular resort for years, being early in the field with holiday bungalows; but it has become famous as the point at which the North Sea Gas is brought ashore to be distributed over all the country by giant pipelines buried beneath Norfolk fields. The ruins of Bromholm Priory lie behind the village. It was an offshoot of Castle Acre priory in 1113, and it was a great place of pilgrimage as it had a reputed fragment of the True Cross.

Bacton Church lies inland, but if we follow the coast road we find that it has to go round the great barn at Paston which is 163 feet long and is the only remaining building from the home of the Paston family. However, Paston Church on our left just before reaching the Barn has several memorials to members of the family. Two of them are by Nicholas Stone. The one to Dame Katherine Paston (1629) has a beautiful reclining figure in alabaster under a canopy in the usual seventeenth-century style. The sculptor was paid £340 for it. Next to it is the memorial to Sir Edmund Paston (1632), but in contrast this is a severely plain urn on a pedestal standing in a canopied recess. The church, like the barn, is thatched. Facing one on entering the South door is a wall-painting of St Christopher 12 feet high and in very good condition. Close to it is the upper part of another wall-painting of the legend of the Three Living and Three Dead Kings. The skeletons are plainly visible. The road passes a well-preserved windmill at the entrance to Mundesley, which is a typical small seaside place suitable for families with children. The railway has gone from the station, with its spacious approach which must have been the scene of many happy arrivals in the early 1900s when it was built. The coast road dips where the stream from a mill-pond runs down to the sea. The mill has been demolished but the mill-wheel is still turned by the water. It is the only overshot wheel in the county.

There is a jingle: 'Gimingham, Trimingham, Mundesley and Trunch, all lie together in a bunch.' Trunch lies grouped round its fine church—a compact little place with a triangular churchyard and a road along each of its sides, the houses and shops looking towards the church. There is a Tudor cottage in one corner of the churchyard and one of the village pubs in another angle of the triangle. The church is the finest in this group of villages. Its font canopy, one of only four of its kind in the country (another is at St Peter Mancroft, Norwich), is justly famous. Eight elaborately carved pillars support a nearly flat vaulted ceiling covered with wooden tracery and above this rise six painted panels which must have once had statues or carvings in front of them, because on one is the outline of a Rood and another that of a Crucifixion scene. Each panel has an elaborately carved canopy above which is a carved finial supported by six carved ogee crocketed arches. There is a carved and painted beam across the belfry arch and the screen, dated 1502, has 12 painted panels of saints. Against the east side of the screen are six misericord seats. There is a fine hammerbeam roof. Outside, an unusual feature is that the middle buttress on the south side of the chancel springs from the roof of a porch built in front of the priest's door.

The next resort beyond Trimingham is Overstrand. This part of Norfolk is sometimes referred to as Poppy Land, though the efficiency of the farmers has reduced the numbers of this picturesque weed. Overstrand is fighting a losing battle with the sea: one by one its houses fall over the tall cliff. The numerous landslides are not entirely due to erosion but partly, here as elsewhere, to the earth being undermined by underground springs which emerge from the cliff face. However, plenty of new building has taken place recently behind the older houses, so their present owners evidently consider that they will at least last for their life-time.

One can walk along the cliffs from Overstrand to Cromer past the lighthouse. Compared with most of the places already mentioned, Cromer has the air of a real seaside resort, with a pier, promenade, shops and amusements. Though most of the houses were built during the past century, there is the nucleus of a fishing village on the top of the cliff lying under the shadow of a great church, with a tower 160 feet high which acts as a landmark for sailors. It is the tallest tower of any Norfolk parish church. Cromer became fashionable as a seaside resort late in the eighteenth century and there are a number of Regency houses on the cliff. It is famous for its crabs and also for its lifeboats.

When the tide is exceptionally low, the beach reveals traces of the past. The stumps of the trees of a submerged forest can sometimes be seen and fossil remains of prehistoric animals have been picked up. In November 1970 the stumps of piles which showed the outline of a former harbour became visible. Little ships from here traded with France from the time of Elizabeth I, but it is not known how long it is since the harbour was destroyed by the sea.

Although cliffs line the coast, the land rises still higher behind Cromer and a ridge runs parallel with the sea a mile or so inland. It is thickly wooded and provides opportunity for walks and picnics. On the top of the ridge lies the Felbrigg estate, recently left to the National Trust by R. W. Ketton Cremer, an outstanding authority on Norfolk in the seventeenth century. The last of his books to be published before his death was *Norfolk in the Civil War*. Felbrigg Hall lies in its park some distance from the road, with only the church for company. The front of the Hall was built about 1620; it was enlarged between 1674-87 and a wing was added in 1750. There is an orangery built in 1704-5. The hall, to the left of the entrance, has some stained glass in the windows which came from St Peter Mancroft Church, Norwich. The hall leads into the dining room which is in the west wing added in 1674, and this in turn to a drawing room which has a wonderful plaster ceiling dated 1687 and which is similar to the plaster work at Melton Constable dating from the same year. A further room was designed to house the pictures brought back from a 'Grand Tour' by William Windham. The Library over the Hall in the south front contains some books which formerly belonged to Dr Johnson.

In the church are some of the finest brasses in Norfolk; the most notable is that to Sir Simon Felbrigg and his wife, dated 1416. She was cousin to Anne of Bohemia, Richard II's Queen. There are memorials to members of the Windham family who owned Felbrigg Hall for generations and they include the work of Grinling Gibbons and Nollekens. Among his many books Mr Ketton Cremer wrote one entitled *Felbrigg* which traces the history of the house and the many generations who inhabited it. It may possibly outlast his other books and take its place with V. Sackville West's *Knole and the Sackvilles* as a model story of a house. He undoubtedly enjoyed living in the house and he has made it possible for others to enjoy it too.

Since the proliferation of caravans on the cliffs at East and West Runton, it is more pleasant to go from Cromer to Sheringham along the road past Felbrigg and the beauty spot known as the Lion's Mouth (how did it get this name?), the British Camp, and the more aptly named Pretty Corner. From these well-wooded spots there are distant views of the sea. A feature of the view is a steep, rounded hill on the cliff below, which is known as Beeston Hump, with the ruins of an ancient priory nearby. Beeston Regis Church, close by, has a fine painted screen. The building stands near the edge of the cliffs and is insured against falling into the sea before the year 2192. It lies immediately to the east of Sheringham, a resort somewhat larger than Cromer but with little in the way of entertainment. It is a popular residential place among retired people and there are several hotels. In contrast to other parts of the Norfolk coast the beach is composed of large pebbles and until recently flint picking was a local industry. There are some longshore fishermen, as at Cromer; in fact there was nothing but a very small fishing village here until the coming of the railway brought development in the latter half of the nineteenth century. The grounds of Sheringham Hall, a mile or more inland, are well worth seeing when they are open in the rhododendron season as one can walk for more than a mile through these flowering shrubs. So many varieties and colours are grown that there is a display of blossom for over three months. The house and grounds were designed by Humphrey Repton and his son John Adey Repton.

Other houses, such as Northrepps Hall and Cromer Hall, show that this range of wooded hills has been a favoured place of residence for a long time. It must be a healthy situation for, a little farther west, still on the Cromer Ridge, at Kelling, there is a group of sanatoria and convalescent homes. One of them, Home Place, was built in 1903 as a very large and unusual private house at the then enormous cost of £60,000. It is described in detail in Nikolaus

Pevsner's admirable volume in the Buildings of England series.

Holt is a little market town which takes its name from the woods which surround it. Here is Gresham's School, founded by Sir Thomas Gresham, the Elizabethan financier who also founded the Royal Exchange. It remained a small country grammar school until about 1900, when it grew into the present large public school. Since then it has had some illustrious pupils, among them Benjamin Britten and W. H. Auden.

The Cromer Ridge provides some of the most beautiful scenery in the county. It is well wooded and in places rises to a height of 300 feet above sea level. Between Holt and Edgefield the road drops steeply and rises again where the moraine of an Ice Age glacier can be distinctly seen. A little to the West, and still on fairly high ground, is one of the great houses which are so plentiful in Norfolk, Melton Constable Hall, is regarded as the finest specimen of the so-called Christopher Wren style of house. The main house, which is of brick and stone, is nine bays by seven and there is a large domestic wing projecting northwards. This wing is basically Elizabethan, though disguised when it was refaced in the early nineteenth century. Inside the house, which has unfortunately not been inhabited for some years past, are some very fine plaster ceilings dated 1687. The house itself was built by Sir Jacob Astley between 1664 and 1670. In the park is an unusual church. It contains Norman work, and a south transept was erected as a family pew in 1681 and contains many memorials to the Astley family who bore the title Lord Hastings. Sir Jacob Astley fought in the Civil War and his prayer 'Lord, I shall be very busy this day. I may forget Thee but do Thou not forget me' is still quoted.

Between Holt and the sea is some wooded heathland where one is free to roam unrestricted by cultivation. The short, but pretty, River Glaven flows through Letheringsett where the Doric front of the Hall close to the road provides an unexpected touch; then continues through the park of Bayfield Hall and over a ford at Glandford where there are two curiosities, the restored church and the Shell Museum, both the work of Sir Alfred Jodrell who lived at Bayfield Hall. The church was rebuilt between 1899 and 1906 in memory of Sir Alfred's mother, and, although small, contains all the features one could find in a Norfolk church, including excellent glass, a wealth of woodwork and a hammerbeam roof. Adjoining the churchyard is a building erected about the same date to house Sir Alfred's collection of shells, chosen more for their beauty or quaintness than for scientific reasons. The museum is open to the public. The whole village bears the stamp of the squire who was responsible for its building and maintenance.

About two miles to the West of Glandford is Langham where, after over 20 years in the Navy during one of the most eventful periods in its history, Captain Marryat settled down to write his popular books including *Mr Midshipman Easy*.

Before entering the sea, the River Glaven passes through the village of Cley-next-the-Sea, prounced to rhyme with 'sky'. It was once a port but is now more than a mile from the sea and has declined. The large church bears witness to its former importance. It lies even farther inland than the little town, overlooking a village green at Newgate. When it was built the harbour must have been a little to the West where the Gaven flows through marshy ground, but embanking prevented the tide from coming in and the town moved its harbour nearer to the sea. This in turn became silted up and the sea retreated still farther away. The town is picturesque and mainly built of flint pebbles and red brick. The houses are well cared for.

Cley Church, with its back to the town, is not impressive in outline but it is extremely rich in detail and even after having viewed it from outside, the visitor will be surprised at its size when he enters. The south porch is richly decorated, and reveals an unexpectedly fine doorway, as also does the west porch. The clerestory windows, alternately cinquefoiled circles and two-light pointed, are unusual and decorative. There is a roofless south transept, known to have been so for over 350 years, and possibly never completed. The tracery of the large four-light south window in this transept is elaborate and unusual. The upper part has an almost square design set on one of its corners. Large crockets adorn the edges of the gable. On entering the church the great width and the large open space at the west end, which is not used for seating, make the building impressive. There are five bays in the nave, which like the main fabric of the building, belongs to the Decorated period. The figures which form the corbels above them are interesting.

The road between Cley and Sheringham is one of the most beautiful stretches of coast road in Norfolk. As we have seen, the salt marshes at Cley are nearly a mile in width but they rapidly decrease in width towards Weybourne where they cease and cliffs continue eastwards. The road follows the edge of the marshes through Salthouse, which was inundated by floods in 1953, and then turns inland towards Weybourne which nestles in a valley. Weybourne Church is mixed up with the ruins of an Augustinian Priory which took over an existing church about A.D. 1200. The portion of the tower which stands at the east end of the present church is of Saxon workmanship and adjoining it and in the farm behind are the ruins of the Priory. The present church is mainly the result of rebuilding in 1866 and 1886 after 300 years of neglect.

Westwards from Weybourne the salt marshes continue for over 20 miles, one or two miles wide, between the road which marks the old coast-line and the sea itself. This is one of the longest continuous stretches of coast under the protection of the National Trust, and Blakeney Point and Scolt Head are nature reserves and the haunt of sea birds—and bird watchers. The numerous creeks provide excellent anchorage for small boats and the area is very popular with yachtsmen. Marsh-samphire grows on the mud-banks and is gathered for use as a vegetable: the soft leaves have a rather strong taste. Sea lavender adds colour to these salt marshes, which are otherwise mainly brown and green.

The little port of Blakeney is one of the most attractive places on the North Norfolk coast. Its harbour and the long channel which connects it with the sea provide ample anchorage for the many yachts and small boats which use it as a base for sailing, and the village attracts visitors and residents. There is a good hotel and a number of detached houses, as well as many old flint-built cottages which have been modernized. Much of this work has been done by a local housing society which has been organized in order to preserve the appearance of the place and to prevent its exploitation and destruction. The very narrow main street runs straight downhill to the quayside, where buildings have been carefully converted into good class shops and flats. Near the quay is a fifteenth-century building, known as the Guildhall, which looks across the marshes towards Blakeney Point. Blakeney Church is on the main road rather detached from the village. It is large and has two towers; the West Tower is massive and 124 feet high, and a slender, square tower at the east end is supposed to have been used for a beacon. The chancel is Early English and stone vaulted, but the remainder of the church belongs to the Perpendicular period.

The marshes continue westward past Brancaster, where there is a network of channels, with the site of the Roman Branodum Camp on the edge of the firmer ground. The marsh ends to the west of Thornham, where there are traces of a tiny port, long abandoned. There is no continuous road or path along the marshes, only straight lanes or tracks at right angles to the coast road ending in culs-de-sac.

The country which lies behind these salt marshes is perhaps most typical of the county. It has a style of its own not shared by neighbours, for it has none, except the Norfolk hinterland. It also has an architectural purity less mixed than in other parts of the county, for the houses are mainly built of flint pebbles and have red or black pantile roofs. These tiles are said to have been brought from the Continent as ballast in the holds of the little ships which sailed to and from the ports along this coast. Until recently, when some modern brick houses have been erected, there has been complete unity of style and colour in the villages and little towns which lie along the coast road. The grey of the flint walls and the red roofs caught in the sunlight, sometimes against a grey background of sea and sky in winter, or contrasted with the green of the grass in summer, impress the eye by their harmony. It is a neighbourhood which attracts people of an academic turn of mind who are seeking quiet, as well as those who have outdoor interests such as bird-watching, sailing and golf.

My first introduction to the North Norfolk coast was on a dark night in the 1930s when I was driven by car along the coast road from Hunstanton to the windmill at Burnham Overy, where I was to stay for the weekend. The headlights of the car, innocent of dipping devices in those days, lit up the village streets so that they looked like stage settings. Awakening on a dull November morning, high up in the windmill, the view across the deserted marshes showed no sign of life; only an upturned boat and the channels between mud-banks covered with coarse grass were visible. In the opposite direction, to the south-east, there seemed little sign of life either. The thick walls of the mill might have been a fortress, or a lighthouse set on land instead of the sea. There was no sound except that of the wind.

Burnham Overy also has a water-mill which belongs to the National Trust. It stands astride the little River Burn at a bend in the road and dates from 1737. The windmill was built in 1814 and looks perfect, with its round brick tower tarred black and its round cap and sails and galleries painted white; but the machinery has been removed.

There are several Burnhams in the group, all with churches, so (as Cobbett used so often to remark) the district must have been more populous than it is today. Burnham Market forms the centre, with its wide main street which must have been the market place, and its shops, and some houses which must have once been shops also. Burnham Westgate is part of the little town; so too is Burnham Sutton. Burnham Overy a mile to the east has a curious church with a central tower which has only quite small doorways in its eastern and western sides leading into the chancel and nave respectively. Burnham Overy Staithe has a tiny harbour, as its name indicates, and is used by yachtsmen. Burnham Norton church has two interesting pulpits; one, dating probably from the fifteenth century, has painted panels depicting the Latin Doctors of the Church and the Donor, John Goldale. The other pulpit, which is in use, belongs to the Jacobean period. Both Burnham Norton and Burnham Deepdale churches have round towers, and the font at the latter is a square Norman one with panels carved with representations of the work of the 12 months of the year. Although the subject is different there is a similarity to a font in Fincham Church in West Norfolk, a good many miles away. The last of the Burnhams is the most famous as it was the birthplace and childhood home of Admiral Lord Nelson; in his last letter, written before the battle of Trafalgar, he mentioned the place with affection. The rectory in which he was born no longer stands, as his father pulled it down and built the present one in 1802. The church contains a number of articles associated with Norfolk's most famous son.

A mile to the east of the Burnhams lies the great park which surrounds Holkham Hall. It covers about five square miles, but the property of its owner, the Earl of Leicester, spreads much more widely. It represents the achievement of his ancestor, 'Coke of Norfolk', that great eighteenth-century agriculturalist who transformed a barren waste into good farm land and who is regarded as the father of Norfolk farming. Coke spread his ideas among the farming community through his 'Sheep Shearings', which were, in effect, the first agricultural shows. Holkham Hall is a Palladian building which might seem more at home in Italy than in the bleak windswept open spaces of the North Norfolk coast. It was designed by William Kent and built between 1734 and 1761. The severity of the grey brick exterior is compensated for by the design and proportions, but the interior is magnificent. Pevsner says that 'it is more consistently palatial than that of almost any other house in England'. The entrance hall, with its great staircase with its pink marble columns and rich decoration, takes one's breath away by its Roman splendour. It measures 46 feet by 70, and is 43 feet high. The state rooms, which occupy the central block, are filled with furniture contemporary with the building and its collection of pictures and statuary rival any great house in the country. The plan of this great building, which is 344 feet long, consists of four oblong blocks at the corners connected with the central block. One of these corner blocks was designed to contain the private apartments, another those for visitors, the third the kitchens and servants' quarters and the fourth the chapel and other domestic buildings. The park and grounds, including the lake, which is about a mile long, were laid out by Capability Brown in 1762.

The town of Wells-next-the-Sea lies to the east of Holkham and is the only surviving port on the North Norfolk coast. Its name is a bit of a mis-nomer for its harbour is over a mile from the coast at high tide and a good deal more than twice that distance from the sea when the tide is low. However, small coasting vessels are to be found moored at its quay and this gives the place the air of a seaport town. Away towards the sea are sand dunes covered with pine trees which were planted by a former Earl of Leicester, making a very pleasant and sheltered beach. Wells preserves the style which we noticed before and which gives North Norfolk its distinctive atmosphere. There is a network of narrow streets and passages and most of the houses are faced with the ubiquitous flint pebbles.

We have followed the coast road, but inland there is a network of lanes which are as pleasant as any one could find. Many of them wind between high banks and some are so narrow that grass grows along the middle of the roadway now that there are no horses to tread it down. It is pleasant, sparsely populated country with scarcely any villages or outstanding features. A few miles inland a road runs from east to west through North and South Creek and Docking towards Heacham, and once a railway did so too. For Norfolk the land is high, frequently rising to over 200 feet above sea level, and this type of country extends some 12 miles south before villages become frequent and the scenery changes. The area includes the largest and most magnificent mansion in Norfolk, Houghton Hall, the palatial home of the Marquess of Cholmondeley and built by Sir Robert Walpole, England's first Prime Minister. The house was started in 1721 and finished when Holkham was just begun.

Houghton Hall was not completed until 1735, although it was in use before that date. Everything is of the best quality. The outside is of Yorkshire stone; inside the doors and other woodwork are mahogany. The stone hall on the first floor is a cube 40 feet by 40. It no longer serves its original purpose, as the flight of stone steps which must have made an imposing approach from outside was lost, it is said, in a wager by the gambler, George, Earl of Orford, who sold much of the remarkable collection of pictures in 1779 for over £40,000 to the Empress Catherine the Great of Russia. They are now in the Hermitage at Leningrad. However, what is left is well worth seeing, although the house is not normally open to the public. Much of the original furniture is still in place. A distinctive feature of the exterior is the four stone domes at the corners.

The church lies in the park a short distance from the Hall, and until 1729 the village of Houghton clustered round it, but Sir Robert built a new village outside the main gates into the park and there it remains till this day, an example of eighteenth-century planning. The new houses were probably superior to the old village, but sentiment led to its being immortalized by Oliver Goldsmith in his poem *The Deserted Village*.

In East Barsham Manor House, which belongs to the early Tudor period; Blickling Hall, which, although built in 1620 may be said to be Elizabethan; and Raynham Hall, which came immediately after Blickling and was followed by Houghton and Holkham, Norfolk can show the development of the architecture of great houses over a period of 300 years, all within an area which can be explored in a single afternoon.

Hunstanton was the first place where I set foot upon Norfolk soil. It was in the spring of 1934; on the day Summer Time began, to be precise; and it was a glorious day. I went by train from Ely, seeing the land rise up to my right as the train ran into Norfolk, with the flat land of the Fen and Marshland on my left. At Wolferton station I was conscious that I was on royal property; everything was in such perfect order, and I recollect that the lamps on the platform had crowns on them. As the train left the station through a cutting in the sand hill, I saw sand martins flying in and out of their nests. Presently there were glimpses of the sea and at last the train stopped at Hunstanton station within a stone's throw of the sea. The place looked bright in the sunlight, the wonderful air filled my lungs and ever since I have found that even a visit of a few hours will do me more good than a week at some other resorts. There was an air of quiet affluence: the hotels, the private schools and the range of substantial lock-up garages provided in a day when the motor car was an uncommon luxury. I was taken for a walk through the gardens on the top of the cliff and looked down upon the rocks below, with their pools and the wide stretch of sand beyond. It is at this time of year and in late September that Hunstanton is at its most pleasant. The crowds are not there, except on Sundays: the Sunday school treats and Mothers' Union parties have not arrived; but the sun can shine as brightly as in the height of the summer and the sight of it setting across the water to the west can be enjoyed at a more convenient hour. Yes, Hunstanton is a west-coast resort in East Anglia, and brought up in the West Country as I was, it felt natural to me for the sun to go down over the sea.

I soon got to know the Hunstanton area well and visited the place frequently during my years at Ely. The red soil and the narrow lanes in the pretty country behind the town reminded me of Devon. The 'ginger-bread' stone of the houses gave an individual character to them.

Old Hunstanton lies at the point on the coast where the aspect is north-west. The Hall belongs to the Le Strange family whose origins go back to before the Conquest. Little can be seen of the Hall which has suffered from fires, but the church of St Mary which stands at the end of a pretty cul-de-sac is worth visiting. Although it was restored in the mid-nineteenth century much remains from the thirteenth century. Among the monuments is a fine brass to Sir Roger Le Strange on a tomb-chest dated 1506. Henry Le Strange Styleman Le Strange, who died in 1862, designed the stained glass in the east window of the south aisle, painted the roof of the west tower, and also designed and painted most of the roof of the nave of Ely Cathedral but died before he could finish it.

Most of Old Hunstanton looks anything but old for it consists mainly of pleasant twentieth-century houses and a fine golf course which stretches along the coast behind the sand hills as far as Holme-next-the-Sea to the east. When the tide is low the sea retreats for a long distance, leaving a very wide extent of glorious sands where there is ample space for enjoyment without intrusion by other people. It is at Old Hunstanton that sand dunes give place to the cliffs which extend along the westward facing coast for a little over a mile. Layers of white and red chalk and red carstone alternate, giving a striking effect which is all the more surprising in a county where there is an almost total absence of rocks of any kind. The cliffs rise to a height of 60 feet and at the foot—fallen boulders and water-worn rocks are formed into pools where crabs and other creatures may be found. There is a common at the top of the cliff. Here a walk gives good views across the sea; by night the lights of Skegness can be seen on the far side of the Wash, and by day it is possible to distinguish Boston 'Stump' some 20 miles away.

New Hunstanton, or 'Hunston' as it is usually called, is no longer the quiet, genteel Victorian resort which was the joint creation of the railway and the Le Strange family in the 1860s and 70s. The railway brought prosperity and between the wars trains poured thousands of visitors into the town during the summer season, at very low fares. To the people of Cambridgeshire, and as far afield as Leicester, it was 'their' seaside resort and many of them still go there, even though the railway has been closed. But although Hunstanton has changed, there is something which cannot be altered and that is the marvellously bracing air. The sight of the sun setting over the sea makes a perfect end to the day (though the reflected light off the water doubles the risk of sunburn). In spite of later additions Hunstanton has a harmony of its own because the development in the town's early days was compact and uniform. The shaft of an ancient cross, moved from Old Hunstanton, stands on the wide sloping green which forms the centre of the town, and it is on this spot that St Edmund, King of East Anglia, is said to have landed just before he became King. There are the remains of a ruined chapel dedicated to him on the cliff near a disused lighthouse.

To the south of Hunstanton, and joined to it by the bungalows which line the coast, is the village of Heacham, no longer what it was, as a result of road widening, though the picturesque Caley Mill still stands among the lavender fields which produce a crop which is made into lavender water and other scented products. Heacham is proud of the fact that John Rolfe, a member of the family who have lived at the Hall for centuries, married the Red Indian princess Pocahontas in 1614. It was she who became famous through saving the life of the explorer Captain John Smith—a story told in most old-fashioned history books. She settled in England with her husband, but died at the age of 22.

The next village south of Heacham is Snettisham, which has become well known through the discovery of spectacular hoards of treasure in the form of Iron Age torcs, or collars, which can be seen in Norwich Castle Museum. These, and much else besides dating from the first century B.C., have been unearthed here. Other finds have been made at Ringstead, a few miles away, where the Peddars Way crosses the downs just before terminating at the sea. In one field at Ringstead large numbers of flint implements have been discovered over the course of years, showing that this area was populated from very early times. It is only in this area of Norfolk that the underlying chalk comes to the surface and produces characteristic downland turf.

Dersingham brings us to the Royal estates which surround Sandringham. Since the property was bought by King Edward VII in 1861, when he was Prince of Wales, this has been a favourite home of the Royal family. Here they could enjoy privacy and country pursuits. It is not an official residence, being the private property of the Queen, and is not maintained at public expense. The gardens are open to the public and much of the estate can be enjoyed as excellent picnic sites have been provided. Many members of the Royal family have been born in York Cottage, which is in the grounds of Sandringham House, and King George V and his son King George VI both died at Sandringham. The estate is excellent shooting country and much of it is farmed. The House itself is by no means a palace, like its near neighbour Houghton Hall, which was considered by King Edward as an alternative before he bought the estate. It is a large country house in Victorian Tudor style and it has been added to from time to time. Some magnificent wrought-iron gates made in Norwich, and given by the County of Norfolk to the Prince of Wales upon the occasion of his marriage in 1863, add a stately touch. The surrounding roads have been planted with trees and rhododendrons, set back behind wide grass verges, transforming the formerly wild heath. Sandringham Church, which lies just outside the private grounds, is a much-visited building. It is built of carstone, very well laid. The building was originally medieval but was much restored in Victorian times. The fittings include a silver altar and reredos and a pulpit of oak and silver, besides other fittings mostly given by an American, Rodman Wanamaker. Some members of the Royal family lie buried in the beautifully kept churchyard, for this is very much their parish. Not only do the Queen and her family attend this church, they take part in the life of the parish and in the activities of the local Women's Institute. The estate includes a variety of scenery: farmland, heather, woods and salt marshes. The Prince of Wales' bride, better known later as Queen Alexandra, loved this place because of its resemblance to her native Denmark.

South of the Sandringham estate is the ancient town of Castle Rising, now a small but very interesting village. It was once a seaport,

19 *Paston: the Great Barn*

20 *Blakeney: Red House from the quay*

21 *Hunstanton Cliffs*

then the sea receded and King's Lynn took away the trade. There is a magnificent Castle built by William de Albini, who married the widow of King Henry I and became Earl of Sussex. It became the property of the Dukes of Norfolk in 1544. The style of the keep is similar to Norwich Castle, and is one of the most elaborately ornamented Norman keeps in the country. It stands in a bowl-shaped depression made by a huge circular earthwork 1,000 feet in circumference, part of which is probably Roman. The ditch is 60 feet deep and the rampart 64 feet high. Although the main roof is missing, there are still a number of rooms under cover. Howard Hospital, a charming group of almshouses founded in 1614, stands close to the Castle. The old ladies who live there amid the original furnishings wear cloaks with the Howard badge, and steeple crowned hats like witches, when they go to church on Sundays.

The church lies on the opposite side of the road and is an unusually elaborately decorated Norman building with a gabled Victorian top to the tower. On the green is a village cross about 20 feet high. From here to King's Lynn the road passes through Ling Common, an area of steep sandhills covered with pretty woods. The sand is exposed in places, so providing much pleasure for children. As a picnic site it is ideal. Here we should leave our circuit of the coast of Norfolk. We are already out of sight of the sea, which is more than three miles away. The coast which borders the southern part of the Wash becomes more and more inaccessible as it turns westwards and merges into the coast of Lincolnshire.

CHAPTER FIVE

Central Norfolk

If May sees Norwich at its best when the city is full of flowers, then the best time to see Norfolk on parade is on the last Wednesday and Thursday in June; for on these two days the Royal Norfolk Agricultural Association's Annual Show is held on its permanent showground at Costessey. Here you will meet more Norfolk people in the course of a few hours than at any other time. The products and the tools of England's largest industry—agriculture—are on display, and some 750 horses, 400 cattle and hundreds of other animals and birds are looking at their best, some of them apparently conscious of the fact. The visitor will enjoy himself, because the Norfolk Show caters for all tastes, and, as a result, it attracts nearly 80,000 people in the two days.

The Royal Norfolk Show prospers at a time when many county shows are in difficulties, and so it should, for were not agricultural shows invented in Norfolk? 'Coke of Norfolk', who became Earl of Leicester, held, as we have seen, his annual 'Sheep Shearings', which were virtually agricultural shows, from 1778, inviting farmers from all parts, including foreign countries, to see how his improved methods of agriculture worked. He had based his methods on the four-course system of husbandry devised at the end of the seventeenth century by the second Viscount 'Turnip' Townshend, whose estates were at Raynham, near Fakenham, not far away. This system (wheat, turnips, barley, clover) improved the fertility of the soil. The turnips were eaten in the fields by sheep who compacted light soil with their small feet while at the same time manuring the soil.

Coke, who inherited a huge estate of apparently barren, sandy soil, transformed it into a highly productive and valuable one. We visit the Holkham estate and its magnificent mansion in another part of this book.

The townsman will probably not realize that he is passing through a highly mechanized industrial area when he motors through Norfolk. He may not even see a single man at work in the fields in the course of the day. But the person who travels along the Norfolk roads regularly throughout the year knows how much is being done. One day, as if some order had been transmitted over the radio to all concerned that morning, every farmer will be found doing the same operation as if by instinct, be it ploughing, drilling, hedging or harvesting. The first fine day after a spell of bad weather will find tractors everywhere, for English farming, and this means Norfolk farming above all, is the most highly mechanized in the world. In August huge combine harvesters drone round the fields, followed by baling machines and sledges to remove the straw, while lorries relieve the combines of their burden of threshed grain, and take it to silos or drying plants.

Early in the season the machinery for harvesting peas and getting them to the frozen food factories within an hour from the time they were growing, moves from field to field; during the last three months in the year the sugar beet 'campaign' is in full swing. Campaign is the right word, for the operation is carefully planned to ensure that a steady uninterrupted flow of beet reaches the factories; the process of converting beet into sugar must go on night and day without a stop once it has begun. One factory may well handle a million tons of beet in the course of three to four months.

Norfolk turkeys have long been famous, but now turkeys are handled by mass-production methods and one firm alone sells a million birds a year. Ducks, too, are bred in vast numbers. Thousands appear to spend their short lives sitting on the ground waiting for the next meal. They are to be found largely on the poorer soil of south Norfolk which they enrich and make suitable for cropping. Pigs and poultry are highly organized, but they are less in evidence because they are kept in buildings. Cattle, though numerous, are not such a familiar sight as in other parts of England, for the Norfolk farmer tends to regard grassland as a luxury when it might be producing arable crops. The permanent pasture land is largely on the marshes bordering the Broads.

The showground at Costessey is four miles from the centre of Norwich on the A.47, which crosses Norfolk from east to west and ultimately finds its way to Birmingham. Like a great many of the Norfolk place-names which seem purposely designed to mislead the visitor, or to act as a shibboleth for the easy identification of the 'furriner', Costessey is not pronounced as it is spelled, but is known as 'Cossey'. The visitor will also look in vain for Windham, Haisbro', Hunston or Hobbis, unless he remembers to follow signposts to Wymondham, Happisburgh, Hunstanton or Haut Bois respectively.

If, to reach the Norfolk Show from Norwich, we had approached the ground by the more pleasant route leaving Norwich at Earlham, we should have passed through the very small but picturesque village of Colney. Here a large group of farm buildings has been converted into modern houses and the village forge into a bungalow, while retaining the original fabric in each case, so that both the plan and aspect of the village have been changed as little as possible. What used to be a beautiful country lane to Cringleford, with fine oak trees on each side, has been widened and largely spoiled for the convenience of some scientific establishments attracted to the site by the University of East Anglia which can be seen across the valley of the Yare; but this road cannot be seen from the main centre of the village. The church has a round tower and a tablet over the porch which records the death of a man in 1806 who was run over by a waggon. Road accidents took place even then! The road continues along rising wooded ground past Colney Hall and a turning soon leads to Bawburgh, pronounced 'Babur' and other variations, which is described in another part of this book, and so to Costessey or to Easton and the Ringland Hills.

The Ringland Hills provide a welcome open space where one may picnic amid surroundings very different from anything in the country west of Norwich. The steep-sided ridge runs from east to west. It is the moraine of one of the glaciers of the Ice Age and consists of gravel deposited by melting ice at the foot of a glacier. There is a similar deposit south of Holt. The north face of the Ringland Hills is quite steep and there is a pleasant view over the valley of the River Wensum which flows at the foot of the ridge, with its quiet mirror-like surface between trees and meadows. The hills are covered with bracken and crowned with birch trees, and where they are crossed by a narrow road from Easton there is an open space which is much frequented. On the south side of the ridge the ground slopes down to the tiny River Tud. The road which formerly ran through a ford, to the delight of children, now crosses the stream by means of a culvert. Towards the east the trees on either side of the valley meet to add a sense of mystery and, on the opposite slope, West Lodge Woods make the road dark as it climbs to join the A.47 at Easton.

Westwards the Ringland Hills turn towards the north, and widen into downland at Honingham; and farther on they lead to Weston Longeville where a disused aerodrome has been converted into an intensive turkey farm and packing station. Huge buildings house many thousands of birds and there are facilities for packing a million of them a year. Before reaching Weston a road runs down the north side of the ridge to the pleasant village of Ringland, whose church is interesting. It has a hammerbeam roof disguised with wooden coving in the same manner as that of St Peter Mancroft, Norwich. The bridge over the River Wensum is a haunt of fishermen and bathers and the road winds up beside the wall of Taverham Hall estate. The Hall is now a private school, noted for its choir. The way continues to the Fakenham road, avoiding the extensive and unfortunate development which has overtaken the rest of Taverham. The road which links Weston with the Fakenham road is pretty, particularly where it passes the Old Hall at Weston, which stands in its moat not far from Lenwade Mill. A mile or so up the Fakenham road is the Great Witchingham Wildlife Park, where rare birds are bred and, in some instances, return to their countries of origin to save their species from extinction. There is an extensive zoo with animals and birds shown in spacious surroundings.

We are now in the valley of the River Wensum which flows across the middle of the county from west to east, combining with the River Yare at Norwich to find its way to the sea at Great Yarmouth. We will return to the Wensum valley later in this chapter, and also to Weston Longeville, but for the present we will re-visit the valley of the River Yare which we crossed at Bawburgh, and explore it.

A glance at a contoured map of Norfolk will show that the river valleys radiate from Norwich and that the main roads run along the ridges between them. The valley of the Yare above Norwich is subject to frequent flooding after heavy rain or snow, particularly above Earlham and Bawburgh, but the minor roads in the valleys have been so sited that they remain above the water level. The road by which we left Norwich continues, after leaving Colney, through some pretty wooded scenery which includes Marlingford Grove, made famous by Crome as the subject of one of his pictures, and after dropping to the bank of the River Yare, follows it to Barford Bridge. Bawburgh and Marlingford lie in the valley out of sight of the main road and they are connected by a minor road. Marlingford straggles along it and its fine white-painted mill stands astride the river making an attractive picture. To the left, a short distance before crossing Barford Bridge, a turning leads to Wramplingham, a pleasant unspoilt village with a number of old houses. The most attractive feature of the interior of the church is the beautiful range of lancet windows in the chancel; six on one side and five on the other.

A succession of water mills can be found at frequent intervals along the remainder of the course of the river and a tributary which flows through Kimberley Park.

Kimberley Hall, built in 1712, stands in its extensive park about two miles north of Wymondham and has been the home of the Wodehouse family for centuries. The Hall is some distance from the road and is not easily seen. However, the pretty village green with its thatched cottages, just off the Watton road, causes one to pause and admire. Hingham, to the west, is a village which was once a market town and has the air of one. There are two greens, one a square, formerly the Market Place, across which the road cuts diagonally. It is surrounded by some good-looking Georgian houses and an old coaching inn with a large effigy of a white hart over the door. As in many places, a few small buildings have sprung up in one corner of the square, doubtless originally market stalls which acquired squatters' rights, and against the wall of one of them is a large boulder presented by the inhabitants of the town of Hingham, Massachusetts, to its English namesake.

In the early seventeenth century there was a Puritan Rector of Hingham, Robert Peck, who proved to be very troublesome to the Church authorities, and to Bishop Matthew Wren in particular. In 1637 Peck left Hingham with a number of people from the village and emigrated to Hingham, Massachusetts, which was already an established settlement. He remained there until 1646, when he returned to Hingham, Norfolk, where he was now safe under the Commonwealth. In the meantime, his son had quite illegally taken his place at the church, but as soon as this was discovered by the authorities the son deemed it prudent to return to Essex, from whence he had come. It was soon after this, in 1637, that Samuel Lincoln, an ancestor of President Abraham Lincoln, migrated from Hingham to America. His father Edward had settled at Hingham after being disinherited by Samuel's grandfather, who lived at Swanton Morley, near East Dereham.

Hingham Church is a fine large building. The east window is of German glass purchased abroad by Lord Wodehouse in 1813. It dates from about 1500 and is reminiscent of the windows of King's College Chapel, though the colouring is paler. On the north side of the chancel is one of the largest and most important monuments in the county. It is of red stone and was erected to the memory of Lord Morley, who died in 1435. The second green at Hingham is irregular in shape and is the site of a fair which is a relic of the days when Hingham was a market town. The side streets are worth exploring on account of their pleasing old houses.

East Dereham, to the north of Hingham, is in the geographical centre of Norfolk, and with a population of over 8,200 is the fourth largest town in the county. George Borrow was born at Dumpling Green, now a suburb of the town. Borrow referred to Dereham as 'Pretty D.', which is hardly how we should describe it today, for it has become a manufacturing town. It has a long history dating back to A.D. 650 when Withburga, a daughter of Anna, King of East Anglia, founded a nunnery here. An elaborate sign was erected across the main street to celebrate the 1,300th anniversary of this event. Withburga was sister to Etheldreda, who founded the Monastery of

Ely. Like her sisters, she was canonized after her death in A.D. 654 and buried in the churchyard, where the well named after her can still be seen a few yards west of the church. In the year 974 the monks of Ely stole the body of St Withburga while their Abbot was entertaining the people of Dereham to a feast, and conveyed it to Ely, mainly by boat through the fens, so that it could be buried beside her three sisters, SS Etheldreda, Sexburga and Werburga, in the Minster at Ely. East Dereham Church stands on a sloping site and the floor follows the slope of the ground. It has a number of interesting features, amongst them a monument by Flaxman to the poet William Cowper, who lived and died at Dereham. At the corner of the churchyard are some pargetted cottages—rather rare in Norfolk —named Bishop Bonner's Cottage. The tower of the church, built in 1501, is detached and stands at a short distance from the east end, possibly because the site slopes downhill towards the west where the soil may be less stable because it is near a stream. This tower was used during the Napoleonic Wars to house French prisoners of war.

Norfolk is a large county and at Dereham we find the parting of the ways between east and west. There are probably many people who seldom go from one side of the county to the other and who may scarcely have visited Norwich in their lives.

The diaries of Rev Thomas Armstrong give an intimate picture of life at Dereham in the mid-Victorian period. A more famous diarist, the Revd James Woodforde, we have already mentioned; 'Parson' Woodforde, who was born in Somerset in 1740 and became Rector of Weston Longeville, mid-way between Dereham and Norwich, in the year 1776, where he remained until his death in 1803. His diary, kept from 1758 till 1802, vividly reflects the way country people lived in the latter part of the eighteenth century. There is a daily account of what Woodforde ate, how he passed his evenings with his niece Nancy, who kept house for him, the social visits paid to neighbouring clergy and gentry, his problems with the village people, and with the day-to-day matters on his land. The occasional visits to Norwich for shopping and to go to the theatre or concerts are also described together with impressions of interesting people whom he met, and there are naïve entries which show his own credulity about cures for the various ailments which worried him. The Rectory in which Woodforde lived is gone, but there is a portrait of him in the church.

The diary of a very different parson in the mid-nineteenth century, and that kept by his patron, have been combined by Professor Owen Chadwick to make that fascinating book entitled *Victorian Miniature* which we have already mentioned in passing. The diarists were Revd W. W. Andrew and Sir John Boileau, who were Vicar and Squire of the tiny village of Ketteringham near Hethersett. Strong characters each of them, they did not always agree. Their story puts the life of this small place under a microscope. Sir John Boileau's predecessor at the Hall was a very different type of person, who was by no means limited to the life of the little place. She was a Drury Lane actress who had performed under Sheridan and married Edward Atkyns, owner of Ketteringham Hall. She and her husband later settled in Versailles and Charlotte Atkyns became acquainted with Marie Antoinette. When the Queen was imprisoned, Mrs Atkyns devoted herself to trying to effect her escape and finally ruined herself financially in doing so. Her attempts to release the Queen read like extracts from *The Scarlet Pimpernel*.

There is a steady flow of Norfolk diaries from publishers, and many other books dealing with highly specialized or localized aspects of Norfolk life, but at any one time not many are in print. The collection of local books in Norwich Central Library is one of the finest in the country and in addition the library has thousands of books which mention Norfolk, if only in passing.

To the north-east of East Dereham is the village of Swanton Morley, which was the home of the ancestors of President Abraham Lincoln. The Angel Inn incorporates part of the house in which they lived in the early seventeenth century. The fine church standing on rising ground overlooking the valley of the River Wensum, was built in the early Perpendicular period. It may have been commenced about 1360 and the will of Sir William de Morley, dated 1379, left money towards the building of the church 'now begun', so work was in progress by that date. There is a record that it was consecrated in 1440. Inside, the Perpendicular arcades soar upwards and the building is full of light. The font stands on a projection from the base of one of the piers which support the lofty west tower. The sound openings in the upper stage of the tower look like four-light Perpendicular windows and are unusually large for Norfolk.

At Worthing, farther to the north, the road crosses the river near a water mill. A short distance from here the Roman road which crossed the county from east to west went over the river by a wooden bridge near the site of which two fine Roman helmets of gilded metal were found. They are to be seen in Norwich Castle Museum. They are in almost perfect condition, but being too thin for protection in battle it is believed that they were worn on ceremonial occasions in the same way that our Household Cavalry helmets are used. One is decorated with an eagle's head and the other with Mars, Victory and Medusa.

North Elmham almost adjoins Worthing and straggles for nearly a mile towards its church. For five years ending in 1971 the site of the vineyard to the west of the church was excavated and evidence of an extensive Saxon settlement was unearthed. Post holes showed that there were a number of buildings, including one 60 feet long and 25 feet wide; there were a great many burials and remains of ditches and a road. To the north of the church the remains of a Saxon Cathedral have been accessible for many years. The walls stand to a height of about 10 feet and the internal length is 123 feet. The original building was of brown conglomerate but there are the remains of a number of additions made by Bishop Despencer of Norwich who obtained a licence to crenellate in 1388. It was he who had the moat dug round the building. The see of East Anglia was moved from here to Thetford in 1075 from which place it was finally moved to Norwich in 1096. The original cathedral consisted of a nave, a T-shaped transept at the east end with a semi-circular apse, and two square towers in the angles between the transept and the nave and a much larger tower at the west end. In the 1960s the title of Bishop of Elmham was revived by the Roman Catholic Church for the assistant bishop in the Diocese of Northampton of which Norfolk was a part.

The remains of the Cathedral should not divert us from looking at the parish church, for inside there are some surprises. Upon entering, a flight of steps leads down into the nave with its thirteenth-century round and octagonal piers. There are also examples of

Norman work, though from outside the church appears to belong to the Decorated and Perpendicular periods.

The next village to North Elmham is Brisley, which has the largest common in Norfolk. The church, which a few years ago was in a deplorable condition, has been put into good repair by the people of the village, an example of what can be done by a small community. It illustrates the transition from the Decorated to the Perpendicular style.

This part of central Norfolk is covered by a network of winding lanes, with undulating farm land interspersed with woods and the parks of country mansions.

A few miles to the east, beyond Bawdeswell, is the little town of Reepham with a nice Market Place surrounded by Georgian houses and the King's Arms inn. On one side in the churchyard stand two churches actually joined together, although they were built to serve the two parishes of Reepham and Whitwell. Within two or three miles of Reepham are two other churches which must be included in the top rank of the 600-odd ancient churches in the county. In fact some enthusiasts claim that Cawston is the finest. Cawston and Salle churches both belong to the same period: the early years of the fifteenth century, but present different appearances. Cawston has a massive lofty tower entirely ashlar-faced, with decorated base courses which run right round even inside the building where the buttresses can be seen at the west end of the nave. The west walls of the nave appear to have been added at a later date and this, together with the fact that the western-most arcade is much wider than the remainder, indicates that the tower was once detached from the rest of the building. The fine west door of the tower seems to lead nowhere, as so many west doors do, but it is well worth examining. The spandrels contain carvings of a wild man and a dragon and these motifs are found elsewhere in the building, for they were associated with Michael de la Pole, Earl of Suffolk, who built the church except for the north aisle which was provided by Robert Oxburgh.

The exterior, apart from the tower, is rather disappointing as the plaster which once covered the rubble walls only remains in patches; inside the effect is fine. The double hammerbeam roof is the chief feature, with angels standing upright on the ends of the hammers. There is a lofty painted rood-screen with doors, probably dating from about 1500, with 20 panels of saints. In the north aisle, which has been associated with the Plow Guild, there is not only an old plough, but the sign of the former Plough Inn at Sygate. The gallery in the west tower has an ancient inscription 'God spede the plow and send us ale corn enow our purpose for to make at crow of cok of the plowlete of Sygate: be mert and glade war good ale yis work mad'. There are many other interesting features in the building.

Salle church has every feature it would seem possible for a church to have, but the proportions of the tower are not so fine as those of Cawston. There are north and south porches, both with rooms over them; spacious north and south transepts, misericord seats in the chancel; a seven-sacrament font with a font-cover suspended from a beam projecting from the gallery in the west tower and many other details. Yet this fine church serves a parish of only 137 inhabitants. An extract from a Close Roll of 1345 gives a clue to the reason why this magnificent building should stand in such a small place. Referring to the Flemish weaving industry in Norfolk it says: 'To the weavers and other workers of Aylsham, of linen cloth of Betele (Bale), or flannel of linen thread of cover-chiefs of Salle'. The latter was a particular make of veil. The ancestors of Anne Boleyn were closely associated with Salle from 1283 onwards; Thomas Boleyn, who died in 1411, is commemorated in a south window, and Geoffrey Boleyn and his wife (1440) have a brass in the nave.

As at Cawston, there are wild men and a griffin on the north porch, but the spandrels of the west door have a pair of angels swinging censers, their bodies covered with feathers.

Heydon, a mile or so to the north of Salle, is a village that has won a prize as best-kept village in Norfolk. It has a pleasant village green with attractive houses and shop fronts and enjoys the additional advantage of being a cul-de-sac and so is free from traffic. The Hall is the home of the Bulwer family, of whom Lord Lytton was a member. He wrote under the name of Bulwer Lytton and his best known novel is *The Last Days of Pompeii*.

The network of meandering roads in this part of the county is matched by the tracks of former railway lines which cross each other and run side by side in places. The former Great Eastern (later the London and North Eastern) and the Midland and Great Northern Joint Railway were in keen competition; each tried to serve every market town and much duplication of services resulted. Cromer, North Walsham, Fakenham, King's Lynn and Aylsham each had two stations apiece, and Norwich and Yarmouth had three stations each, though Victoria Station Norwich ceased to be a terminus for passengers during the Great War.

The disused embankments and cuttings and the stations which have been put to other uses are fascinating to the student of industrial archaeology. At one time Melton Constable was a miniature Swindon, with the works of the M. & G.N.R., but the whole system, which extended from Great Yarmouth to Leicester, was one of the first casualties of the railway closures.

The northern part of central Norfolk which we have been looking at is very pleasant country, quiet, restful and well wooded, with pretty river valleys. The central part of southern Norfolk is different and flatter; not so picturesque, and devoted to intensive arable farming. The country lying south of Attleborough and Wymondham as far as the Suffolk border between Harleston and the Lophams, which I took as the eastern boundary of Breckland, is of this nature, so it is not an area to visit for its scenery. However, its architecture and historical associations certainly repay a visit.

At South Lopham the source of the River Waveney and the River Little Ouse sends its water eastwards and westwards from a point crossed by the road which leads to Redgrave. South Lopham Church, with its massive Norman tower, stands in a beautifully kept churchyard. The tower dates from the same period as the tower of Norwich Cathedral and is decorated in a somewhat similar manner. The lofty north wall of the nave must be Saxon, for there is an unmistakable Saxon window high up near its western end.

Turning north through the straggling village of North Lopham, we can visit East Harling and Kenninghall. The former has a striking church, with a spire which may have been the inspiration for the somewhat similar one which was added to St Peter Mancroft, Norwich, in the nineteenth century. Like St Peter Mancroft too, East Harling has old stained glass. Near the church stands an ancient dovecote. East Harling, though only a village of 930 inhabitants, has the air of a small market town, with a market place and a number of shops. In 1840 it had 1,062 inhabitants and boasted a proportion of professional and business people which it certainly cannot support today. The former shops, now used as private houses, illustrate the change. Kenninghall, three miles to the east, has declined even more, from a population of 1,389 to 780, in the same period of 120 years. It lost its chief glory long ago: there is now no trace of Kenninghall Palace, the former home of the Dukes of Norfolk which was taken from them by Henry VIII and given to the Lady (later Queen) Mary, his daughter. Kenninghall has associations too with another much earlier Queen, Boadicea, who is supposed to have lived at Candle Yards near Kenninghall Palace. A rectangular enclosure with earth banks is visible on the site. Adjoining Kenninghall is the pretty park of Quidenham Hall, now a Carmelite Priory but formerly the home of the Keppel family whose head was the Earl of Albemarle. It was purchased by the third Earl in 1762 and the Hall was remodelled apparently about that time. Glimpses of it may be seen from the road across the land which is farmed for the nuns by a steward. A chapel and other buildings have been added, and a guest house, in which one could spend the most peaceful holiday imaginable, has been contrived out of some domestic buildings. The ancient village church stands with its round Saxon tower in a pretty setting by the road.

To the east of Quidenham is Banham, another small village with a planned air. In front of the church is a square green, lined with tall trees with some picturesque shops and houses. Old Buckenham, some two or three miles to the north, is built round a large village green which is more like a common.

New Buckenham, close by, owes its origin to the fact that the Castle was removed there from Old Buckenham by William II de Albini, who built it between 1145 and 1150. It stands on the west side of the village on a mound some 40 feet high and is surrounded by a moat filled with water. The remains of the stone keep stand inside the ramparts on the side farthest from the present entrance and are remarkable for being the first round keep to be built in England and possibly anywhere in Europe. The walls of the keep are

11 feet thick at the base. The Castle was demolished by the owner, Sir Philip Knyvet, a Royalist, during the Civil War, possibly under pressure. He was imprisoned by the Parliamentarians for some time and his letters to his wife during his detention have been published. The chapel of the castle, which also served as the village church until the present much larger building was erected at the opposite side of the village in the second half of the fifteenth century, still stands at the entrance to the lane which leads to the Castle. It is now used as a farm building. New Buckenham was planned and built as a direct result of the building of the Castle and is a good example of medieval town planning on the grid system, which was used for other new towns laid out in the same period. There is a square green which used to be the market place with a picturesque market house supported on pillars, with some interesting carving which looks as if it might formerly have been on a house front beneath a window like the examples to be seen at Clare in Suffolk and Newport in Essex. Most of the houses date from the eighteenth century, but the original plan of the streets has been retained. To the east of the village lies a large common, but the country in this direction is flat and unattractive.

Although the country round new Buckenham may be uninteresting, once we have crossed the common on the road to Norwich and have reached Bunwell, the road follows a route along higher ground and the villages and roadside farms hide the less interesting land behind them. The road undulates and winds through well-wooded country and is a more pleasant and quiet route between Norwich and Bury St Edmunds or Thetford than the more popular trunk roads. The road passes through a succession of villages and one is closer to the essential life of Norfolk than is the traveller on the main roads. A tall television mast guides one to Tacolneston (pronounced Tacolston if you have to ask for it!) where there is a picturesque farmhouse built of brick and half timber, three storeys high, with gables and a projection at the back which rises straight out of the stream by which the house stands. It is as delightful and unexpected as it is unlike anything in the neighbourhood, and this adds to the charm. There is a pretty bend in the road as it passes between the Church and the Old Hall. On the left of the road just before a turning leading to Ashwellthorpe, is a rather charming inn and a few miles farther on, beyond the oddly named village of Bracon Ash, we come to the wide common, round which Mulbarton is built. On its far side there is a curious monument in the chancel of the church. It is made in the form of a metal Bible which can be opened to reveal a poem composed by her husband, in memory of Mrs Sarah Cargill who died in 1680.

Only a short distance beyond Mulbarton is Swardeston, where a short lane to the west leads to the church, which has been restored and put into thorough repair in the 1960s. Through a Tudor brick porch one enters a thirteenth-century nave without aisles, a curious feature of which, defying explanation, is the range of round-headed recesses in the walls. There is some nice stained glass and a seventeenth-century font cover. The chief interest, however, is the association with Nurse Edith Cavell, whose execution by the Germans in 1915, for assisting Allied soldiers to escape from Brussels, aroused such indignation that it has not been forgotten yet. Her father was Vicar of Swardeston for 46 years and he built the present Vicarage in which Edith Cavell was brought up. Looking at it one thinks how many learned, brave and courageous people in our nation's history have come from houses like this; people who have set an example by their strength of character in the way in which Edith Cavell has done. At the centenary of her birth and fiftieth anniversary of her death, in 1965, a re-assessment of her life made it clear that she could well have been famous for her pioneering work in nursing had the manner of her death not overshadowed her work. The country vicarage or rectory has also been the source of much research and learning; it is to the Revd Francis Bloomfield, Rector of Fersfield, near Diss, that we owe the most noted history of Norfolk, which he published in the eighteenth century.

Beyond Swardeston is Keswick, where the New Hall has been greatly enlarged and converted into a College of Education, both Keswick New Hall and the Old Hall have been the homes of the Norwich banking family of Gurney, who settled here in the early nineteenth century. The Old Hall can be seen across the fields which rise to where, at the top of the hill, stands tiny Keswick Church in a grove of trees. Upon closer inspection it will be seen that it consists of a small round

22   *Castle Acre Priory: the west front, c. 1140-50*

tower and a very small nave, restored in the 1890s, but the chancel is in ruins. A minute sanctuary was added in the 1960s. Over the brow of the hill the road descends to merge with the main road from Ipswich and Colchester to cross Harford Bridge into Norwich.

The main A.11 road from Newmarket to Norwich runs roughly parallel with the route we have been following and, after leaving Thetford, it does not pass any towns or villages until it reaches Attleborough, which need not detain us except for its church, which has a magnificent screen and rood loft which is painted with the Arms of the 24 episcopal Sees established when it was built. Some of the building is Norman, including the lower stage of the tower which is at the east end and now serves as the sanctuary.

Between Attleborough and Wymondham, at Morley, is Wymondham College, a very successful educational experiment. It is a large boarding school run by Norfolk Education Committee and about 700 boys and girls from all parts of Norfolk have the advantage of facilities which a scattered community can only obtain by long journeys daily to the nearest grammar school. The houses are built with dormitories for small numbers and the common rooms are modern and cheerful.

Wymondham is a busy market town with a population of over 6,000. It is consequently large enough to provide most of the amenities as well as the essentials of life. In a town like Wymondham there is so much going on that one could hardly be dull. The construction of a by-pass road has taken the intolerable burden of through traffic from the centre of the town and has benefited business.

Although many of the shops and houses have modern fronts they have old beams inside, for many date from the time when the town was largely rebuilt after a fire which destroyed more than 300 houses, on 11th June 1615, while most of the inhabitants were at church. It was at this time, in 1618, that the picturesque Market Cross was rebuilt. It is octagonal and timber-framed; a room on the first floor is reached by an outside stair, while the lower storey is open on all sides. It is crowned by a pyramid roof. The emblems of the town—a wooden spoon and a spigot crossed, derived from the old industry of wood-turning—appear in the wood carving round the building. Brush-making has taken the place of wood-turning as

23 *Raynham Hall: middle of west front commenced in 1622*

the chief industry. There is a Bridewell with the cell windows still barred, built in 1787, and the Public Library is housed in the four-teenth-century Chapel of St Thomas à Becket, which for many years was part of the local Grammar School, now defunct. Next to the Library is the half-timbered Green Dragon, one of the oldest inns in England.

It is the Abbey which dominates the town with its two lofty towers, one at each end. The Abbey was founded by William de Albini in 1107 as a daughter church to St Albans, for the Benedic-tine order. The present church incorporates nine bays of the Norman nave and has a fine hammerbeam roof with many angels. On the north side is a fifteenth-century aisle with another very fine hammer-beam roof, an ancient font and a hanging brass candelabra dated 1712. This aisle alone is larger than many churches. There is also a smaller post-reformation south aisle. A gallery in the huge west tower houses an organ given in 1793, and the church has one of the finest and largest choirs in Norfolk. But the most striking thing is the modern reredos. It was designed by Sir Ninian Comper, to-gether with the tester over the high altar and the rood at clerestory level. The reredos has 14 carved, gilded and coloured figures in gilded niches and the colour and gilding continue to the rood and the angels with six wings which stand above the tester. At the end of a service during which he had been gazing at it, a small boy turned to me and said 'I think heaven must be like that'. No doubt the architect would have felt that his work had succeeded if he had heard that remark.

As in other monastic churches where the nave was used by the parishioners, there was friction between the monks and the towns-people. The two towers are a lasting reminder of this, for the larger and more massive west tower was built by the parishioners about 1448 and a number of legacies in the next few years con-tributed towards the cost. It is 142 feet high and contains a fine peal of bells. The other tower, now at the east end, but once the central tower before the Reformation when the choir, transepts and monas-tic buildings were destroyed, was built by the monks about 1400. Church life at Wymondham, as in the other leading market towns in Norfolk, is flourishing. The Abbey is no museum piece but a really live church. It is a very large parish (the second largest in England) covering 10,000 acres and has daughter churches in out-lying neighbourhoods.

To the south, on the Suffolk border, is the market town of Diss. This busy place serves as the centre for a wide area and in a survey a few years ago was found to do more business per head of popula-tion than any other town in the county. The chief feature of Diss is the Mere, a lake round which the town is built. There is an import-ant poultry market, and, like Wymondham, the chief industry is brush-making. The vista up the main street looking towards the church, which stands on rising ground, is striking. There are several timber-framed buildings, some with good carved corner posts, not-ably one with a scene of the Annunciation at a house in St Nicholas Street, but interesting buildings of all periods abound.

Two miles to the east of Diss, where the road which follows the River Waveney crosses the main road from Norwich to Ipswich, once the Roman road from Venta Icenorum (Caistor St Edmunds) to Camulodunum (Colchester), is Scole, where a very fine coaching inn, the White Hart, stands near the crossroads. It is of red brick, with five Dutch gables, and was famous for an elaborate sign which spanned the road and cost £1,057 to erect in 1655, when the inn itself is supposed to have been built. The sign was destroyed round about 1780, but prints of it survive. The road between here and Norwich runs through the rather flat and featureless country already described, until it reaches Long Stratton, whose name de-notes both that it stands on a Roman road and that it has what is termed a 'street' plan, otherwise ribbon development along the sides of a main road. The church has two curiosities: a clock on its round tower with only one hand—presumably exact time did not matter when it was put there—and a prayer wheel, a device which was used in the Middle Ages to determine the day on which to start a course of prayer. Near the church is a rather gay-looking modern police station, so different from anything else in the village.

The most interesting buildings in the triangle bounded by Scole, Long Stratton and Bungay are the windmill at Billingford, which has been put into order and preserved as a good example of a Nor-folk tower mill, and Shelton Church, some two miles south-east of

Long Stratton. The church is a fine example of late Perpendicular work and was built by Sir Ralph Shelton, who, in his will dated 1487, ordered the church to be completed in the same plan as he had begun it. It is of red brick ornamented with stone and blue brick, with a clerestory and a vestry at the east end behind the altar. The church has been thoroughly restored and contains monuments to the Shelton family.

From Shelton we can continue south to Harleston, a small market town on the Norfolk-Suffolk border close to the River Waveney. Although Harleston is an old town its mother church is at Reden-hall, a small village a mile and a half to the north-east. There are some old houses at Harleston including the seventeenth-century Swan Inn with an attractive wrought-iron sign. Redenhall Church has one of the finest towers in Norfolk and it is even more impressive through standing on rising ground. The tower was commenced in 1460 but a rebus of shell-tun which appears on it indicates that it was not finished until 1520 during the incumbency of Thomas Shel-ton, who became Rector in 1518. The date 1616 which appears on the tower refers to repairs which were effected after the tower was split during a tempest. (The word 'tempest' is still used by Norfolk people to describe a severe storm.) The tower is covered with flint flush-work panelling and has massive polygonal buttresses at the corners rising to pinnacles. Inside the building there is a good deal of woodwork, much of it Victorian.

The road continues to Bungay which stands on rising ground with the River Waveney flowing round its western and northern sides through meadows which are subject to flooding. Facing Bungay across the river from the Norfolk bank is Ditchingham, with its associations with Sir Rider Haggard: a Norfolk man, he settled at Ditchingham after his return from Africa and took a great interest in agriculture. His daughter, Lilias Rider Haggard, also an author, lived in a house not far from Ditchingham House which her father formerly occupied. Ditchingham has been the home since 1858 of the first order of Anglican nuns to be founded since the Reforma-tion. The Community of All Hallows runs schools and among other activities has maintained a mission in Norwich and cares for St Julian's Church there. Ditchingham Hall is a handsome house standing in a park landscaped by Capability Brown. The Hall dates from 1702 but has a modern façade, built in the style of that period from mauve and red brick. The ground falls away steeply from the Hall to a lake set amid woods.

The triangle: Norwich, Long Stratton, Loddon, contains some of the most pleasant countryside within easy reach of Norwich, so much so that it is becoming increasingly popular for residential purposes and is likely to lose the very charm which has attracted people to it. It is higher ground than most parts of Norfolk, rising to 220 feet above sea level at the Railway Inn at Poringland. Why this inn was so named is a mystery, because it was always remote from any railway line and is likely to remain so. The area includes the valley of the little River Tas, which flows northwards to join the River Yare at Norwich. This valley has provided some of the most interesting archaeological discoveries in the county and appears to have been favoured by prehistoric man, the Romans and the Saxons. The churches are small but all have interesting features. The area has its complement of country houses, most of them of moderate size, only Shotesham Park being of particular note. It was designed by Sir John Soane about 1785 for a member of the Fellowes family whose descendants still live there. The house and its surrounding park look like a setting for a Jane Austen novel. The country lanes in this area are very narrow and provide pleasant walks and there are a number of commons which enable the pedestrians to leave the roads. Dunstan Common is a particularly popular picnic spot. There is another large common at Fritton and another at Saxlingham Green, and, although a little outside the boundaries I have chosen, a large common at Mulbarton which has been improved and cared for by the inhabitants. It is a well-wooded countryside and in the Bergh Apton district, particularly, holly trees with thick trunks stand in the hedgerows and attain a size comparable with other trees. At Framingham Earl rhododendrons flourish and at Framingham Earl Hall there are some fine trees planted by Dr Edward Rigby, who lived there in the early nineteenth century. The epitaph on his grave in the churchyard reads:

A monument to Rigby do you seek?
On every side the whispering woodlands speak.

A large grave outside the east end of the church also commemorates the quadruplet children of Dr Rigby, none of whom survived more than a few weeks. The doctor practised in Norwich at Rigby Court, St Giles Street, where, at one time, John Crome acted as his errand boy. He must have been one of the first commuters to have lived as far as five miles out of the city. In his young days he was visiting Paris on 14th July 1789 and recorded his impressions of the crowds after the storming of the Bastille. 'Such an instantaneous and unanimous emotion of extreme gladness as I suppose was never before experienced by human beings...' But presently another procession produced a different response: 'A deep and hollow murmur at once pervaded them, their countenances expressing amazement mingled with alarm for carried on two pikes were the bloody heads of the governor of the Bastille and the Prébôt des Marchands who had tried to prevent the people from arming themselves.'

The church at Framingham Earl is small; its chancel is mainly Saxon. The rest of the building is Norman. It has a round tower and is of flint with as little other building stone as possible. Even the corners of the nave are built of very large blocks of flint. There are round double-splay windows. A curious feature is that the building tapers somewhat towards the east end. The Norman doors, particularly the south door, are fine specimens of their period.

Framingham Pigot Church is Victorian, but the village is pretty and unspoiled. Both the villages owe much of their charm to the fact that they belong to the occupants of Framingham Pigot Hall and Framingham Chase, who do not encourage development. Poringland, the neighbouring village, is a complete contrast and an unfortunate example of what unrestricted development can do to a village. Brooke is another rapidly growing village, but it has retained some of its old character in its centre. Kirstead Hall, on the southeastern boundary of Brooke, is a fine specimen of a Jacobean brick farmhouse dated 1614. The country between here and Loddon is pleasant. Where council houses have been built they are the work of the Loddon Rural District Council and are modern, original and attractive.

To the west of the Norwich-to-Bungay road the land falls rapidly to the Tas valley. At the Norwich end of this valley, between Trowse and Arminghall, the site of a Wood Henge—a timber version of Stonehenge in a county devoid of stone—was discovered some years ago by aerial photography. There was a circle of great posts each about three feet in diameter with an earthen bank round it, but little can be seen from ground level. This road leads, after two miles, to a much more tangible ancient monument, the site of the Roman town of Venta Icenorum, which means 'the market place of the Iceni'. It was the administrative centre for the region and was first laid out on the banks of the River Tas in about A.D. 70. The massive town walls were not built till about A.D. 200 and consisted of a ditch 80 to 100 feet wide, with a wall built of flint rubble 11 feet thick and faced with squared flints and brick. There was a gate in the middle of each wall and bastions at intervals. The ditch and the bank on which the wall stood still survive, 1,100 feet long from north to south and 1,400 feet from east to west. Some portions of the wall itself remain and the area enclosed is 35 acres. Excavations have revealed the plan of the town, the sites of the public buildings and the industrial area; it was one of the few Roman towns in Britain where glass was manufactured and there was a woollen industry. The town was occupied by the Romans for nearly 400 years. They must have been very fond of oysters judging by the number of shells I have found there just outside one of the gates. The village church stands in the south-east corner of the site of the Roman town inside the ramparts. On the hills on the opposite side of the valley a Saxon cemetery was discovered when the railway was constructed.

There are three churches, one of them ruined, and some picturesque houses at Shotesham. Beyond this village to the south are the equally pretty Saxlinghams. A fine timber-framed Old Hall of the Elizabethan period stands just outside St Mary's Church at Saxlingham Nethergate. Here and to the south are many cottages and farmhouses with plastered and whitewashed walls in the Suffolk style: one just off the Norwich to Ipswich road near Swainsthorpe might well have appeared in one of Constable's pictures. In spite of the superficial resemblance between these buildings, details of style can be distinguished if they are studied carefully. I remember a local architect describing them in a lecture and commenting that a farmhouse in a particular place was built in a foreign style, adding that he meant this in the Norfolk sense of coming from the next parish but one. Between these timber-framed and plastered houses of south Norfolk and the flint houses of the northern part of the county there is an area with no predominant style, and too many buildings which are a red-brick, doll's-house type—two windows and a door on the ground floor and three windows above, with no attempt at ornamentation: no doubt a consequence of the rise in the rural population in the middle of the nineteenth century. The cottages of that period are often in rows of four or more and are of cheap brick construction. However, some of both these types of houses have been transformed into modern homes satisfactorily, inside and out.

CHAPTER SIX

Shrines and Pilgrims

On account of its associations with pilgrimages the district round about Walsingham is known as the Holy Land of Norfolk. Walsingham lies to the north of Fakenham some six or seven miles from the sea, and is unique in England. There are two Walsinghams, Great and Little, and in the perverse way common in Norfolk, Little Walsingham is the larger of the two, and was, indeed, a market town. For much of the year it is one of the quietest places one could imagine, but during the summer, and especially on Whit Monday, it is crowded with thousands of pilgrims. Whether or not one is interested in the pilgrimages and the Shrine, Walsingham is a place well worth visiting. It lies in a pretty situation in the valley of the River Stiffkey, which flows northwards towards the sea, and the parkland belonging to Walsingham Abbey adds to its beauty. The little Common Place in the centre of the town has a sixteenth-century brick conduit standing in the middle of the road with an iron cresset—a primitive form of street lighting—on top. All the buildings round it, ancient and modern alike, combine most pleasingly. Some are stone, some brick, some half-timbered, but they blend well. A tiny Shire Hall has its little court room, and in the High Street is the massive fifteenth-century gatehouse of the former Priory, now known as the Abbey. Behind the shops in the High Street is a Market Place, and beyond it again the ruins of Greyfriars, founded in 1347. Down a turning at the end of the High Street is St Mary's Parish Church. The original building was burnt down in 1961, except for the tower and the outer walls, but the new building shows what modern craftsmen can do. It is light, airy and colourful and contains the remains of monuments and brasses which survived from the fire. Fortunately the Seven Sacrament font, one of the finest specimens of this Norfolk type, received no more damage than it had already suffered through the centuries. It was at this church that the cult of Our Lady of Walsingham was revived in 1921 by the Vicar, the Revd Hope Patten, who had a statue of Our Lady made from a representation of her on the old seal of the medieval Priory. This statue was placed in the Parish Church, and in 1931 it was transferred to the present Anglican Shrine which had been built for it outside the walls of the Abbey grounds a little to the north. Built of red brick, in an Italian style with a campanile, it is unlike anything else in Walsingham, but inside it has an 'atmosphere' reminiscent of what churches were like in the Middle Ages, with plenty of colour and everything fresh and new. We are so used to seeing *old* churches, where even if any colour remains, it is faded and fragmentary, that we forget how bright churches once must have been.

The origin of the cult of Our Lady of Walsingham dates back to about the year 1061 when Lady Richeldis, the wife of a Norman knight, Sir Geoffrey de Faverches, who had already settled at Walsingham before the Norman Conquest, had dreams or visions of the Virgin Mary, who told her to build a replica of the Holy House at Nazareth in which the Annunciation took place. This she did on a site in the grounds of the present Abbey near two wells which may still be seen. In 1153, her son, another Geoffrey, founded a priory for Augustinian Canons, who took the shrine of the Holy House under their protection, and it became one of the most popular places of pilgrimage in England throughout the Middle Ages, attracting pilgrims, even from Europe, up till the Dissolution of the Monasteries. A long list of kings, including Henry VIII, came here, and it rivalled Canterbury in popularity. Since its revival in 1921, it has attracted increasing numbers of pilgrims; more than 100,000 visit this out-of-the-way village every year. It can be a moving experience to enter the life-size replica of the Holy Sepulchre in the beautiful grounds of the Pilgrimage Church where there are also three full-sized crosses standing on a mound nearby.

As we shall see, the presence of the original Shrine at Walsingham had an influence on Norfolk and led to the building of a large number of religious houses on the pilgrim routes. The nearest of these was, of course, the Friary in the town itself, which was founded in 1347 and is now in ruins. About a mile to the south, near the banks of the river at Houghton St Giles, there is the fourteenth-century Slipper Chapel. Pilgrims removed their shoes here and walked barefoot for the last mile of their journey to the Shrine. Since the Reformation it had fallen into disrepair and only survived by being turned into a farm cottage, but in 1934 it was restored to its present condition and opened as the Roman Catholic Shrine of Our Lady. The river is crossed near the Slipper Chapel by two or three fords which connect the roads which run alongside either bank. Since the closure of the railway, the road on the east bank has been widened and has lost its pleasant rural character. It is on this road, a mile farther south, that another of the series of houses in Norfolk, which so well illustrate the development of English domestic architecture, stands. East Barsham Manor is best approached from the south; when upon coming over the brow of a hill, one is suddenly brought face to face with its richly decorated red brick and terracotta front. It was built about 1520, but there are parts which could well be earlier. The front presents an irregular range of windows, battlements, Tudor chimneys built of ornamental patterned bricks, and pepper-pot turrets or finials. There is a projecting porch in the middle of the front and opposite it, but several yards away, an elaborate detached gatehouse with the royal arms carved in brick over the arch. It is a building in character with the robust flamboyance of Henry VIII, who stayed in the house when he visited Walsingham, and there are marks inside the building which indicate that Cardinal Wolsey and his retinue probably stayed here too. The house was very carefully restored in 1938 and it is well cared for by its present owners, but it is not open to the public.

Before exploring the pilgrims' way farther to the south, some of the other religious houses which are within easy reach of Walsingham are worth visiting. Bromholme Priory at Bacton has been mentioned in my survey of the coast. It was a popular place of pilgrimage and may well have been visited by pilgrims at the same time as Walsingham. Binham Priory is much nearer and is remarkable in that the west front is the earliest surviving example of the Early

English style, as it was built before 1244. Unfortunately much of the west window has been bricked up, but the tracery and arcading remain. The site of the priory buildings has been excavated and is kept in the swept-and-garnished manner associated with the Ministry of Works. One can reconstruct the life of the Priory from the remains of the domestic buildings round the cloister. The nave of the Priory Church has continued in use as the parish church, although it stands outside the village.

To the west of Walsingham there are remains of small priories at Burnham Overy and Burnham Thorpe near the banks of the little River Burn, which flows through a valley parallel with that in which Walsingham lies. The higher ground between the two valleys is largely occupied by Holkham Park, surrounded by its belt of trees, but the remainder is bare and bleak. The pair of villages, North and South Creake, are in the shelter of the valley of the River Burn, which runs alongside the road. The church at South Creake is large and light and full of interesting fittings. The chancel roof unfortunately provides a discordant note.

The roads from Walsingham and the Creakes converge at Fakenham, a busy market town which stands on the River Wensum. Here, as in several other East Anglian towns, one of the chief industries is printing, with an emphasis on book printing. As over the border of Suffolk at Beccles and Bungay, and of course at Norwich, there is a firm of printers who work for many of the leading publishers in England. Fakenham serves as the centre for this part of Norfolk for shopping, entertainment and education, and of course as a market and provider for the needs of the farming community. It is dominated by a fine church tower, but the centre of the town is not improved by the design of one of the banks.

The route from Fakenham to Norwich along the Wensum valley follows some of the most pleasant scenery in Norfolk. Following the pilgrims' way, we turn south-west and pass Raynham Hall, the seat of the Marquis Townshend, whose ancestor was the 'Turnip' Townshend who, as we have earlier seen, was one of the great agricultural pioneers of the eighteenth century. Raynham Hall, one of the great houses of Norfolk, was commenced in 1622. A part of it is sometimes attributed to Inigo Jones, though there is no proof that he was the architect. The front, which looks down an avenue towards West Raynham church, has three picturesque gables in the Dutch style, with pediments instead of the more usual curved tops. The interior of the house was remodelled about 1720-30 by William Kent. These alterations were made for the second Viscount, who married a sister of his neighbour, Sir Robert Walpole of Houghton Hall. The family were also connected by marriage with the Windhams of Felbrigg.

The road leads on to Castle Acre, which is described elsewhere in this book. The Priory had a large guest house and was a stopping place for pilgrims, who may also have visited West Acre Priory, the ruins of which stand some two or three miles to the west. Here we can find a number of fords through the River Nar, which flows in the direction of Pentney, where there are the ruins of yet another priory with a fine gatehouse, and on to King's Lynn where the Red Mount Chapel was one of the stopping places for pilgrims from Lincolnshire and the west. Other religious houses which catered for the pilgrims and have vanished, were at Flitcham, Rudham and Attleborough. It would be easy to transfer the setting of Chaucer's *Canterbury Tales* to the pilgrims' way to Walsingham. After all, the reeve came from nearby.

> *He came, as I heard tell,*
> *From Norfolk, near a place called Bawdeswell.*

Bawdeswell is on the road from Fakenham to Norwich, and in the village street is a timber-framed building named Chaucer House. Opposite this house is the church which comes as a surprise as it is in the nature of an eighteenth-century revival, built of red brick and stone. However, it dates from shortly after the Second World War, during which the previous church was damaged by aircraft. Today's pilgrims come mainly by motor coach, missing the opportunity to tell each other tales or to observe the details of the countryside. The walker will find the Peddars Way, which passes through Castle Acre on its way to Holme-next-the-Sea, a ready-made route. This section of the track could not have been used by pilgrims, as is sometimes suggested, as it does not lead in the direction they wished to go; but the southern section from Castle Acre to near Stanton in

Suffolk, may well have been followed by them. The Way is much older than the foundation of the shrine at Walsingham, and runs straight as a die across the whole width of the county. Apart from Castle Acre, it does not pass through any villages and for the most part is remote from habitation. It is certainly Roman, as the *ager*, or bank, upon which it was made, can be distinctly traced throughout most of its length, but it is possible that the route itself may be partly that of the prehistoric Icknield Way which forms the basis of another Roman road which takes an almost parallel course and has been traced only a few miles to the west of it, converging with the Peddars Way at Holme-next-the-Sea.

Another lesser place of pilgrimage in the Middle Ages was Bawburgh, where a local saint was buried. St Walstan was a Saxon of noble birth who was born in this village, the son of Benedict and Blide. He went to work on a farm at Taverham in the next valley some four or five miles to the north. He was respected by his fellow workers who regarded him as holy, and was reputed to have worked a miracle upon one of them. His master gave him a yoke of oxen and when Walstan was dying in 1016, he asked that when he died his body should be put on a cart and be buried where these oxen took it. His wish was respected and the oxen went towards Bawburgh, crossed the river and paused at a spot where St Walstan's Well is to be found in an orchard belonging to Church Farm; they then started to mount the steep hill, but finally stopped where Bawburgh Church now stands. When we look at the site we can hardly blame them. Here, in the chapel, now demolished, on the south side of the church, St Walstan was buried. His picture, with his emblem of a scythe, is to be found in several Norfolk churches. The water from the well is supposed to work miraculous cures, and there was a revival of interest in it for a time in the early 1950s.

Bawburgh Church stands on the outskirts of the village on its hillside and is picturesque, with its round tower capped by a conical roof; a wooden gilded flame rises from its apex, giving it the appearance of a candlestick. Whether this was intentional is hard to say, but the present 'flame' is a renewal, and the old piece of carved wood can be seen inside the church. There is also the original rood beam. Bawburgh Hall has been demolished, but there are two small stone buildings in the former grounds, built in the Jacobean style, one of which is known as the Slipper House, probably for the same reason that the Slipper Chapel at Houghton St Giles has gained its name, from the assumption that pilgrims walked barefoot from it to the shrine. As the Bawburgh buildings certainly date from well after the date of the Reformation, this cannot be correct. They are quite unusual for Norfolk and remind one of the type of building one would find at, for instance, Chipping Camden in Gloucestershire. The village has managed to retain its character, and is dominated by its Mill past which the river rushes. The settlement is on rising ground on both sides of the river, joined at the narrowest point of the valley by a hump-backed bridge.

Norwich had its own saint, St William, whose story has been thoroughly investigated by M. D. Anderson in her book *A Saint at Stake*. His death on Good Friday, 24th March 1144, served the two-fold purpose of increasing anti-semitic feeling in the city and providing the Cathedral with a much needed saint to attract pilgrims.

A more worthy religious figure in Norwich, who has not, however, been given the title of 'Saint', was Mother Julian. This remarkable lady lived from about 1342-1430. She was an anchoress and dwelt in a cell attached to St Julian's Church in Norwich, from which she took her name. She was probably educated at Carrow Abbey close by. She had a series of visions and recorded her meditations on the visions she had received under the title *Revelations of Divine Love*, a book which is still read to such an extent that it has been published as a Penguin Classic. It is a work of profound religious thought and in a literary sense is remarkable, not only as one of the earliest English books to survive, but as being by a *woman* living in a period when few people were educated. St Julian's Church was almost destroyed by bombs in 1942, but its reconstruction incorporates all that remains of the ancient building. The site of Mother Julian's cell is now a side chapel. She lived here with a servant and a cat, which appears in a stained-glass window of her in the Cathedral. During her lifetime many people came to her for help and advice, including another woman author, Margery Kempe, who was a native of King's Lynn and was given to more voluble expression of her beliefs than that of Mother Julian's serene writing.

CHAPTER SEVEN

Breckland

In dividing Norfolk into regions for the purpose of this book, it has not been difficult to decide where to make arbitrary boundaries. Inside the county, as in England itself, it is the strongly contrasted areas which help to make travelling so pleasant. In some places as, for instance, on the borders of the Fens, a change of level of less than ten feet can change the scenery and the methods of agriculture, but elsewhere the transition can be blurred by cultivation or by the intervention of patches of soil which differ from the predominant geological formation.

Breckland is a large and highly distinctive region in the south-west of Norfolk. It covers some 400 square miles, about one-third of which lie in Suffolk. We are not concerned here with the Suffolk boundaries of this area, but in Norfolk the western boundary runs in a fairly straight line from south to north, from Mildenhall and Lakenheath in Suffolk to Castle Acre, following the edge of the chalk which underlies most of Norfolk. Here the chalk is divided from the Fens by a band of greensand, carstone and gault along which the A.10 route from London to King's Lynn runs and continues to Hunstanton. What makes Breckland so distinctive is that the chalk is over-laid by a layer of wind-blown sand which in time past made it a veritable desert. Where cultivation has taken place the ground is covered with innumerable flints turned up by the plough. This is the broken land which gives the name 'breck' to the area. For ages the area has been unproductive, its villages isolated and poor, the land given over to heather and rabbits, but it is of great interest to naturalists. Botanically and zoologically it is a countryside unique

24 Breckland: Bodney Warren

in England. The flora and fauna have been left undisturbed, and there are mysterious meres or lakes which have a reputation for appearing or disappearing as a result of changes in the level of the water-table in the soil.

Descriptions of the Breckland of the past give a picture of a desert of sand which made travel very difficult. The Revd Dr Stakeley, a friend of Revd Francis Bloomfield, the historian of Norfolk, wrote in 1745: 'Scarce a tree to be seen for miles, or a house, except here and there a warren house or eminence. I observed many barrows, and now and then some ancient boundary ditches.'

At one time, drifting sand was so serious that in 1688 several houses were engulfed at Santon Downham, near Brandon, and the Hall, demolished in 1922, still showed marks near the eaves where the level of the sand had been. Towards the end of the eighteenth century, enclosures resulted in pine trees being planted to define boundaries and to provide wind-breaks, and the building of large country houses for shooting parties in the Victorian period also resulted in improvement to the estates. However it was in 1922, as a result of a realization during the Great War that England was too dependent upon imported softwood, that the Forestry Commission began planting conifers round Thetford on a large scale. The process still continues, with the result that Thetford Chase is the largest man-made forest in Europe. The effect has been to stabilize the soil, preventing the sand from drifting and encouraging a build-up of humus. Conifers were chosen as being the only type of tree which would grow initially under the prevailing conditions, and the criticism is true that where planting has been intensive the effect can be monotonous. The trees have been planted in straight lines equidistant from each other, usually in 25-acre blocks divided by broad rides to help reduce the risk of fire spreading from one block to another. One can see through the woods in any direction, and look along vistas of semi-darkness to the daylight far away. The air is still and there is no sound of birds, but an occasional squirrel or other animal may be seen or heard. Red deer may sometimes be seen grazing in the fields bordering upon the forest, but they are not descended from the red deer which lived in the region in prehistoric times. In many places, particularly near railway lines and roads,

25   *Swaffham: market cross (1783) with the tower of Swaffham Parish Church*

there is variety, as deciduous trees have been planted to reduce the risk of fire, and these provide a change of colour, particularly in spring and autumn. Mile upon mile of impenetrable dark woods can be sinister. The public are not allowed to wander indiscriminately, but pleasant roadside picnic sites have been provided, and official camping sites are being developed.

The forests are not by any means the only trees in Breckland. Planting began about 200 years ago, to provide windbreaks, and also along the sides of the roads. Many of these old trees remain, with twisted, contorted trunks, to remind us of the power of the wind in this once very exposed area. Their appearance may remind us of the trees which Arthur Rackham used to draw in book illustrations and one can imagine the sinister Rackham faces peeping at the passer-by and thrusting out clawing hands to grasp him. In the days of horses it must have been an adventure to cross this country, either on horseback or by coach, for highwaymen used to frequent Bridgham and Larling Heaths. There would be little sense in calling for help in such places.

The climate of Breckland was, and still is to an extent, that of desert areas—one of extremes of heat and cold with low rainfall. In some years the moisture evaporated from the soil is greater than the rainfall. In frequent journeys across the Breckland in different directions I have noticed that there is a perceptible change of weather when one reaches its boundaries. This is more noticeable when there is wet weather to the south of Barton Mills, or west of Brandon or King's Lynn (which, after all, is only a short distance from the northern edge of Breckland). Norfolk as a whole to some extent shares this wide variation of temperature, but nevertheless I prefer it to the so-called 'milder' climates, which usually produce more rain and snow.

The eastern boundary of Breckland is blurred and my remarks about the transition from rain to fine weather have less application. At Hockham and Larling, ducks have been farmed on a large scale on poor land, thereby enriching it and making it suitable for cultivation. A little to the north, just outside Watton, is Wayland Wood, which is reputed to be the scene of the famous nursery tale about the Babes in the Wood. The ballad from which the tale is taken gives Norfolk as the setting, and it is said that Wayland is a corruption of the 'wailing' which was associated with the death of the children. However, it may be the other way round! Griston Hall nearby was the reputed home of the Wicked Uncle and once had carvings in it depicting incidents in the tale.

The road from Watton to Swaffham provides a view, towards Cockley Cley, of rolling country with patches of forest, in contrast to the typical arable land, plentifully provided with hedgerow trees, which lies behind one. At South Pickenham the road crosses the Peddars Way, that very ancient track which makes its determined but leisurely way across Norfolk from south to north and reaches the sea at Holme. The little River Wissey flows beside it at this point, bordered by wild rhubarb such as John Sell Cotman would have drawn, and the scene, with the brown walls of South Pickenham Church set against a background of dark trees and the old brick wall of the gardens of the Hall in the foreground, has the very tones of his water-colours.

Besides the trees another great change has come to Breckland. Much of it has been taken over by the Army and Air Force. There is the Stanford Battle Area north of Thetford which was occupied for troop-training during the Second World War and has never been released. Now that the army can no longer train on the North-West Frontier or in other outposts of the Empire, they and the troops of our allies can do so here under realistic conditions with live ammunition, in an area of 20,000 acres closed to the public. The inhabitants have had to leave the villages and the churches stand deserted while tanks rumble by and aeroplanes roar overhead, and at night flashes from gunfire are seen in the sky. Permanent army camps lie on the fringe of the area, while farther to the west are large American air bases at Lakenheath and Mildenhall, the R.A.F. aerodrome at Marham and another R.A.F. establishment at Watton to the east.

Industry has followed the forest and on the Norfolk side of the railway, between Brandon and Weeting, are a number of factories which use wood as their raw material. Pit props, wooden lasts for shoes and sports gear are some of the products. One of the oldest industries is here too: charcoal burning. At Thetford there is a hardboard factory.

Industry of all kinds has come to Thetford in a big way. At one time it was an oasis in the desert, quiet, and dreaming about a past greatness in Saxon times when it was one of the most important towns in England, and when from 1075 till 1091 it was the seat of the Bishop of East Anglia before the see was transferred to Norwich. Soon after that event, a great priory grew up and flourished until the Dissolution of the Monasteries. Its Castle, which was demolished in 1173, has left a huge, impressive steep-sided mound rising from a dry moat and these earthworks may have been here before the Normans made use of them, for they dominate the place where the Icknield Way crossed the rivers Thet and Little Ouse. The 20 churches have dwindled to three, with even the threat of further reduction, but the town has retained its Mayor and Corporation. In terms of building material Thetford is untypical of Norfolk so far as its older buildings are concerned, for many of them are of a hard type of chalk, though the Bell Inn at the crossroads is half-timbered. This old part of the building now forms the nucleus of a large modern hotel. Opposite the Bell is the King's House, now occupied by the local Council. Originally the manor-house and the seat of the Earls Warren, it passed to the Crown as part of the Duchy of Lancaster and became a royal residence. Henry i, Henry ii, Elizabeth i and James i occasionally resided here, but the latter sold the property. It had been rebuilt in the reign of Queen Elizabeth and altered in the eighteenth century. In front of it stands a gold-painted statue of Tom Paine, who appears to have been the only man of note produced by the town and hardly one to be proud of, as he sided with the revolutionaries of both America and France against his mother country.

In the 1950s, Thetford became an 'overspill town', taking some of the surplus population from London, together with industries to give them employment. When building started it was found that the remains of the Saxon town were just below the surface and these were carefully excavated and recorded before building proceeded. A picture of life in Saxon Thetford was built up more complete than any previously known. The impressive remains of Thetford Priory have been excavated by the Ministry of Works, who now care for them. Although of little architectural value, they show a very good plan of a typical monastery. One feature which does not seem to have survived elsewhere is the little cloister of the monks' infirmary complete with its cobbled paving. There is also the vault of the tomb of the Dukes of Norfolk. Ruins of other religious houses at Thetford have also survived. A short distance along the Brandon road is the well-preserved ruin of a fifteenth-century house, Thetford Warren Lodge. In the town is a small museum in a timber-framed house, which contains a collection of objects illustrating prehistoric Breckland and medieval Thetford. The town itself has been transformed by development. There is an attractive shopping precinct by the river bank, better in design than in the use to which it has been put. It stands at the confluence of the Rivers Thet and Little Ouse after they have run side by side between tree-lined banks reminiscent of the Backs at Cambridge.

Not far from Thetford is situated one of the most interesting sites in Breckland, if not in the whole of Norfolk. This is Grimes Graves; Grime being a local name for the Devil, who has in the past been credited with the origin of unaccountable natural or artificial features in the landscape in all parts of England. The 'graves' are a large number of depressions in the ground and have nothing to do with burial. Here we can step back into the remote past in a more satisfying way than in many of the other great prehistoric monuments, for the world of today cannot intrude when we explore one of the 'graves'. We leave one of the roads which run either from Brandon or Thetford to Mundford, go for a short distance along a minor road and turn off this along a track which takes us to a clearing in the forest where the only building to be seen is the hut which protects the custodian and houses some objects found in the 'graves'. Some 366 depressions in the ground are the partly filled-in shafts of mines dug by neolithic man 4,000 years ago. The miners were evidently skilled specialists at their job.

Only during the past century have the graves been excavated and their true nature and purpose discovered. About 2330 B.C. early man discovered a seam of very good quality flint near the surface on this site and excavated it to make flint implements. The seam sloped downwards, so that the surface deposit became worked out and it became necessary to dig deeper and still deeper pits to reach it. Two of the deepest and latest pits dating from about 1740 B.C. have been excavated and roofed with concrete so that it is possible to inspect them. The public may descend to a depth of about 30 to 40 feet by means of iron ladders. At the bottom galleries radiate in all directions, dug by the prehistoric miners to enable them to reach the best quality flint, now called 'floorstone'. These galleries sometimes connect with others radiating from neighbouring shafts. It is evident that the supply of floorstone was running out, and a small female figure carved from chalk and placed on a kind of altar with an offering of deer-antler picks has been interpreted as a plea to a goddess when the flint ran short. As one stands in the quiet of the mine one wonders what sort of men worked here, what language they spoke and what standard of living they enjoyed. A diorama, perhaps one-third life size, in the Castle Museum at Norwich, shows one of these miners at work. He is hacking at the flints with an antler pick to remove them from the chalk and his elbow is bleeding from a knock on the stone. A light flickers from a lamp, probably burning tallow, the soot from which has been found on the roofs of the passages. This is one of a series of dioramas showing what Norfolk looked like in prehistoric times, right back to the time when elephants and other wild animals roamed the land. In the Bronze Age diorama we see a smith at work melting the metal to make tools, and in the Iron Age one there is a reconstruction of life at Warham Camp, near Wells. St Edmund, King of East Anglia, being captured by the Danes, is the theme of another diorama in the series.

A considerable industry was carried on at Grimes Graves in making and disposing of flint implements, arrow heads, etc. The Icknield Way, that great highway which connected Norfolk with the centres of population in Wiltshire in prehistoric times, and marked out the route of the present A.11 and its continuation along the edge of the chalk escarpment from Royston to Wallingford, was used by the people of those days when they moved northwards in the summer, and then took the opportunity to buy their implements while they were in the neighbourhood. A chemical technique has recently been perfected by means of which the source of flint implements can be traced; this indicates that the implements travelled a considerable distance from the place where the flint was mined.

All this is remote, but contemporary too. At Brandon men are still working in much the same way as their ancestors 4,000 years ago, for between Brandon and Santon Downham, flint is mined from pits by hand, though by a slightly different method, and it is 'knapped' in a yard behind the public house appropriately named the Flintknappers Arms. Here men take large stones about the size of a ham and after looking at them to find the correct spot strike it with a hammer, dividing each stone into flakes for flint-lock guns, or pieces to make or repair walls, especially the beautiful 'flush-work' patterns to be found on the walls of ancient churches. These present-day workmen can reproduce implements similar to the genuine prehistoric ones. Trade was booming here during the Napoleonic Wars, when large quantities of gun flints were required, and till recently there was a demand from Africa when the natives were only able to obtain flint-lock guns. Should our civilization be in some way utterly destroyed, it would surely be here, if anywhere, that a fresh start would be possible in making tools from natural materials by the unaided work of men's hands.

Near to Grimes Graves is Weeting, with the remains of its castle standing in a moat. It was here that William the Conqueror encamped when he was trying to wipe out the last resistance of the Saxons under Hereward the Wake. Hereward came over from Ely, disguised as a potter, to spy on the Norman camp, but owing to the fact that he had one brown eye and one blue eye, he was recognized. However, he escaped. In those days the fens were undrained; it was only possible to get from Brandon to Ely by boat through devious channels, and there is still no direct road.

At Swaffham, as at Thetford on the other side of Breckland, there has been an awakening too. Swaffham is a market town on a main road, which, by reason of its very large Market Place, has for a long time been a stopping place for long-distance traffic. Swaffham has something which Thetford lacks—style. The Market Place is roughly triangular, with roads branching out of each corner, and it is surrounded by a number of Georgian houses and the Grammar School, the Headmaster's House of which bears the date 1736. The Market

'Cross' is in fact circular, with a lead-covered dome and a statue of Ceres on the top. It was erected by the Earl of Orford in 1783, and is not only elegant in itself but set off to the best advantage. As in many market places there is a group of shops which must have begun as market stalls and acquired squatters' rights, developing into permanent buildings. They are grouped in a higgledy piggledy fashion towards the north side of the triangle. The Assembly Rooms and the Corn Exchange form part of the group. A short lane on the east side leads to the very fine Church standing at the end of an avenue of tall trees. The church was built in the fifteenth century, and unlike the majority of Norfolk churches is mainly of Barnack stone. There is a tower built in 1507-10 with a decorative Georgian spire—there is a very similar one at Necton about four miles to the east—but the angel roof and the soaring Perpendicular arcade of the nave impress one most. Some carved bench-ends depict a little man and a dog on a chain and remind us of the story of the Swaffham Tinker. John Chapman lived at Swaffham in the fifteenth century. He dreamed that if he went to London he would meet someone on London Bridge who would tell him how to make his fortune. He set out for the capital and sure enough he met a man who said that he had had a dream about a certain John Chapman at a place called Swaffham in Norfolk, who, if he dug under a tree in his garden would find a pot of gold. Naturally John Chapman took the hint and the story goes that he found the money and out of it paid for the building of the north aisle of the church. He must have been a wealthy man. I like to think that the story is a parable teaching us to do the work which comes to hand rather than try to make money by going farther afield. It may be that it was the cultivation of his own land which brought Chapman his fortune.

The shops of Swaffham are attractive, and one even displays the Royal Warrant. There is much afforestation round about, but the patches of wood are scattered. Pheasants abound, and one comes across the high hedges grown to provide cover for the 'guns'. There are some pretty villages with equally pretty names, such as Cockley Cley (pronounced as in the other village in Norfolk, to rhyme with 'sky'). Cockley Cley lies to the south-west of Swaffham and has recently been made more interesting by the restoration of St Mary's

Church which is believed to have been built about A.D. 628, thus making it one of the oldest churches in the country. About 1540 the church was converted into a house for the parish priest and a number of alterations and additions were made. It remained in occupation until 1948 and in 1968-70 these additions were removed and the building put into a good state of repair. A few yards from St Mary's is a forge built about 1450 and later converted into two cottages. The original rooms of the forge have been restored and furnished so that the forge itself looks as it would have done soon after it was built, and the living room as it might have appeared about 100 years later. The upper rooms have been converted into a museum.

Across the road from the forge is the site of an Iceni village, and in 1971 a replica of what this village must have looked like in the time of Boadicea has been erected—a vivid lesson in history. A palisade is surrounded by a ditch and the latter is crossed by a drawbridge. The chief's house stands round the trunk of a tree and there is a communal house and individual huts. A spring gushes out of the chalk and this is protected by a small building. It is this spring, one of the sources of the River Wissey, which gives the name to the village, for variations of the words 'Cockley' and 'Cley' occur in other parts of Norfolk where streams are, or have been. Part of London Street, Norwich, used to be known as Cockey Lane from the fact that a stream once ran down it. Cley-next-the-Sea stands on a stream. The road which separates the Iceni village from the forge and St Mary's was part of the Icknield Way and beyond the little Saxon church is the site of a Roman settlement. The Roman road which ran across Norfolk from east to west crossed the Icknield Way at Cockley Cley and this naturally attracted a settlement.

A road continues westwards from Cockley Cley between an avenue of the old twisted Breckland pines to one of the sights of Norfolk which should not be missed. It is the earliest in date of the sequence of great houses in the county. Oxborough Hall, built in 1482, and owned by the National Trust, is a splendid example of the transition from the fortified to the purely domestic manor house. It is of red brick and stands in a wide moat, with the impressive towers of the gatehouse rising 80 feet above the water. Originally built round the four sides of a courtyard, the south range was demolished in 1778, but from the front this is not apparent. Although the gatehouse and the eastern side of the front were designed apparently for defence the remainder could not have stood up to attack against the weapons of the time when it was built, for there are some contemporary windows facing outwards which are too large for defensive purposes. The Bedingfeld family who built the house and have continued to live in it till the present day, remained Roman Catholics throughout, impoverishing themselves by paying recusancy. A good example of a 'priest's hole', or ingeniously designed hiding place, which the agile visitor may enter, may be seen in a small room leading out of the principal bedroom. In the grounds is a Roman Catholic chapel, built in 1835, with some interesting furnishings of foreign origin. The family tombs are mainly in the Bedingfeld Chapel of the parish church. One morning in 1948, without warning, the lofty tower of the church collapsed, destroying much of the nave of the building at the same time. In due course the rubble was removed, leaving the ruins and the untouched chancel which is still used for services. The Bedingfeld Chapel on the south side also escaped damage and has since been carefully restored. The tombs are unusual in being built in the Italian Renaissance style in terra cotta. An example of this material of the same period and possibly from the same source is at Wymondham Abbey. Both date from the early years of the sixteenth century.

The country beyond Oxborough to the west is not attractive. Although the soil is better than the Breckland which it borders, it is flat and the cottages look poor. Buildings which were once thatched are now roofed with corrugated iron or allowed to fall into ruins.

Another excursion from Swaffham, this time to the north, brings us to Castle Acre, a village which stands alone, still stately and dignified in the quiet repose of old age and decay. The church is largely of Saxon origin and so was there before the castle and the Priory and the village. Rolling countryside surrounds Castle Acre in all directions: large fields, with circular copses here and there. The little River Nar flows through the valley to the south and the ruins of the Cluniac Priory stand by its side, almost astride it where the builders diverted the stream to provide the site with water and drainage. At the opposite end of the village is the great castle mound, one of the largest and finest in England. Early in 1971 the Ministry of Environment began preservation work on the Castle, which had been neglected for many years. The thick growth of trees and weeds which covered the whole site was removed, disclosing the very deep ditch and the earth ramparts which surround the inner bailey. The huge mound upon which stood the circular keep, 160 feet in diameter, can now be seen with a substantial length of its wall in better repair than would have been thought possible by anyone who had known the site before. There are other remains of buildings and the Ministry intend gradually to excavate and restore the whole area, which encloses 15 acres.

At the top of Bailey Street is a well-preserved gateway with two round towers which formed part of the Castle. On the opposite side of the main street is an old inn with the unusual name of 'The Ostrich'. The fine church is on the way to the Priory. Two features of interest are the font, with a very lofty font cover, and a doorway on the south side of the building, tall enough for a horse and rider to enter. A lane leads through a fairly well-preserved fifteenth-century brick gatehouse to the Priory. Castle Acre was granted by William the Conqueror to one of his followers, William de Warenne, who was created Earl of Surrey. He introduced the Cluniac order of monks into England and his son founded this priory in the latter years of the eleventh century. Sufficient is left of the great church to show what a magnificent building it was, with its elaborately arcaded front and columns in the nave decorated in the same manner as those in Durham Cathedral. So much of the priory remains that the layout can easily be followed. Some of the later buildings which form the Prior's House remained in occupation until early in the present century, so are well preserved. The whole Castle Acre estate was bought from the Howards, Dukes of Norfolk, by Coke of Norfolk in the eighteenth century. There is a tale which says that Coke owned so much land that the King said he must not buy any more, but when Coke asked if he might buy one more acre, the request was granted. He bought Castle Acre; some 3,000 acres!

Another tale says that the land round Castle Acre is not so fertile as it might be because it has been cultivated for such a long continuous period. The Peddars Way passes by and this track, though used by the Romans, probably dates from before their time. It is evident that the land is not so valuable as in some other parts of the county, for farmers do not plough up to the edges of the roads and there are wide grass verges to the lanes which are a boon to the horseman, for this is the country of the West Norfolk Hunt. It is shooting country too, with plenty of cover provided by high hedges. In some ways this is the most unspoiled part of the county.

There are facilities for walking which are so lacking in the more intensively farmed areas, including the 21-mile stretch of the Peddars Way from Swaffham to Holme which is now in public ownership.

Within sight of Castle Acre, less than a mile to the east, is the Saxon church of Newton-by-Castle Acre with a massive central tower with a pyramid roof. The church at Dunham Magna a farther three miles to the east, is mainly Saxon in style and there is also Saxon work at East Lexham to the north of it.

The River Nar flows through South Acre and West Acre after leaving Castle Acre. South Acre Church has a number of interesting architectural features dating from different periods, including a hammerbeam roof. There is a fine brass to Sir John Harsick and his wife dated 1384 and an elaborate alabaster monument of the seventeenth century to Sir E. Barkham and his wife.

At West Acre there are the remains of a priory incorporated in farm buildings with the fourteenth-century gatehouse standing close to the west end of the parish church. Facing the gateway is a picturesque timbered and weather-boarded house, more in the Sussex style than that of Norfolk.

There are fords across the river which flows briskly over the stones. The rivers of West Norfolk have a steeper gradient than those of the eastern part of the county, which are sluggish and appear hardly to move at all. The Nar gives its name to Narford and Narborough and finds its way to King's Lynn before joining the Great Ouse estuary.

One characteristic of Breckland is its emptiness. The visitor from abroad, or from more densely populated parts of Britain, exclaims with surprise at seeing so few people when England is supposed to be an overpopulated country. But Breckland is not alone in this, for the same might be said of much of Norfolk.

CHAPTER EIGHT

King's Lynn and the Marshland

King's Lynn, at the southern end of the Wash, is the third largest town in Norfolk and is a most interesting and attractive place. Unfortunately the passing motorist sees only the least attractive aspect, for the A.10 from London goes through an industrial estate and modern suburbs on its way to Hunstanton, and the A.47 from the Midlands to Norwich gives a view of a cemetery and factories. At the point where these two roads intersect there is a glimpse of the South Gate, the only surviving medieval entrance to the town, and if a detour is made through it for about half a mile the result is most rewarding.

This ancient town and seaport is the natural centre for the western half of Norfolk and the Marshland, and for centuries was the gateway to the Midlands for commerce with the Continent. It was formerly known as Lynn Episcopi—Bishop's Lynn—but under a charter granted by Henry VIII the name was changed to the present King's Lynn. An earlier charter was granted by King John when he visited the town in 1205; he stayed there again in 1216. It was in that year, when he left the town on his journey to Newark where he died, that King John lost his baggage in the Wash. Numerous unsuccessful attempts have been made to locate the treasure; it is believed to be buried somewhere near the road to Sutton Bridge, in the vicinity of the Walpoles. The Corporation of Lynn has, amongst its regalia, a loving cup gilded and enamelled with hunting and hawking scenes known as King John's Cup, although in fact it probably dates from a century later than his time. The King John Sword, which is probably medieval, and a number of other interesting articles of plate are kept at the Guildhall, which was built in 1421 and has an Elizabethan extension at the side; both parts of the building present fronts to the street of flint and stone in a bold chequer pattern. A further extension at the back of the building, added in 1766, provides handsome reception rooms.

The Guildhall faces the irregularly shaped Saturday Market Place, one of the two market places in the town. On its opposite side, facing the Guildhall, is St Margaret's Church, founded by Bishop Herbert de Losinga, first Bishop of Norwich, and the lower parts of the western towers date back to the twelfth century. The remainder of the building belongs to different periods; the strange impression given by the interior of the nave is due to the fact that the gothic arcades were rebuilt in 1745-6. The church has two of the largest and most famous brasses in England, both of Flemish workmanship. One commemorates Robert Braunch, who died in 1364; on it is engraved a scene showing a banquet given by Braunch to King Edward III in 1349 at which a peacock is being served at table. The other brass, to Adam de Walsokene and his wife, is dated 1349 and has a scene at the bottom showing corn being carried to a post mill.

On the outside of the lower part of the west towers are several marks recording the levels reached by flood water on notable occasions, including the 1953 inundation by the sea which affected the whole of the East Coast. A terrific gale coincided with a high tide and raised the level of the water in the North Sea to an abnormal height. From Yorkshire down to the mouth of the Thames the sea swept across low-lying stretches of coast and broke through weak spots in the sea defences, while the gale lifted off roofs of buildings and carried them, in some cases intact, for a distance. Whole wooden buildings were lifted up and moved, and a number of lives were lost. Communications were destroyed, so that the extent of the damage was not known for a time and rescue was impeded.

During the Middle Ages, Lynn was one of the most important seaports in England, having the advantage of being a gateway to the Midlands. Goods could be trans-shipped and taken inland by water as far as Cambridge. There was trade with the Hanseatic League of the Baltic, and in the street leading to the river opposite St Margaret's is a Hanseatic warehouse. It faces the side of a courtyard of medieval buildings, named Hampton Court, which has been carefully restored and converted into pleasant modern houses. Beyond it is the Greenland Fisheries Museum, another link with the sea. Two sons of Lynn sailed with Captain Cook on his voyage of discovery in the Pacific. The third in command (who, when Captain Cook was murdered by natives, and his second in command died, had to take command of the *Resolution* and bring her back to England) was Captain James Burney, son of the famous musicologist Dr Charles Burney; and the midshipman was George Vancouver, who gave his name to the city in British Columbia. Vancouver was appointed to command an expedition to explore the north-west coast of North America in 1790.

Dr Charles Burney was a musician, at one time the organist of St Margaret's Church, where the organ which he played, built by Snetzler in 1754, is still in use. He was the author of *A History of Music*, and of a journal of his travels in Europe while seeking material for the *History*. He was a man of great energy and talent and had six clever children, James and another son and four daughters of whom Fanny is famous as the first really notable English woman novelist. (Her novel *Evelina* is of course a classic.) Her *Diary* is one of the great English journals and tells a good deal of the circle of Dr Johnson, who praised *Evelina*, and of life in the court of George III when Fanny was a Keeper of the Robes to Queen Charlotte. There is a touching description of the King during his distressing illness. Fanny Burney married a French *emigré*, General d'Arblay, and the journal continues in a French setting and includes a description of Brussels during the battle of Waterloo.

King's Lynn was the one place in Norfolk which saw action during the Civil War. Norfolk was part of the Parliamentary Eastern Association and Oliver Cromwell lived at Ely on its western borders, so it was cut off from the rest of England. Many of the gentry and others were loyal to King Charles, though some families even were divided in their loyalty. In 1643, the Royalists declared King's Lynn for the King and Sir Hamon L'Estrange of Hunstanton became

Governor and put the town in a state of defence. The Duke of
Manchester, for the Parliament, blockaded the town on the south and
Parliamentary ships in the Wash succeeded in preventing all but
one ship from bringing help from the sea. The defenders hoped to
be relieved by the Earl of Newcastle and his Royalist troops in
Lincolnshire, but Newcastle did not come. The defence made sorties
which alarmed the Roundheads, who sent to the Eastern Association
for help and the town was bombarded continually from West Lynn.
After a month, the defenders capitulated in order to avoid bloodshed
among the civilian inhabitants.

The overall character of the centre of King's Lynn has remained.
From across the River Ouse the view from West Lynn reminds one
of Vermeer's 'View of Delft'. The land is flat. The towers of St
Margaret's and the spire of St Nicholas stand above the old ware-
houses and there is a break in the quayside where the Purfleet Quay
leads to the Customs House, a beautiful building erected in 1683 and
designed by a local architect, Henry Bell, who was responsible for
several other buildings which survive in the town. A statue of King
Charles II stands in a niche in the upper storey of the Customs
House, facing the street. Whole streets have maintained their
character without the intrusion of modern buildings. The Tuesday
Market Place, whch covers three acres, is certainly one of the finest
market places in England and it has a Continental atmosphere. It is
surrounded by fine buildings, the best of which is perhaps The
Duke's Head Hotel, also designed by Henry Bell. On market day the
square, filled with stalls, is a sight that should not be missed. It
reminds one of the description of a market in J. B. Priestley's *Good
Companions*. I have seen a man selling 'lino, not oilcloth', and a
stall with an assortment of bicycles, or rather halves of bicycles,
which looked as if they had been culled from wayside pits, in addition to the dealers in clothes, plants and other goods found in most
markets.

Lynn Mart is a fair which fills the Tuesday Market Place from
St Valentine's Day, when it is opened by the Mayor, for a fortnight.
It is the first fair in the showmen's calendar after the close season
which follows Christmas.

In the far corner of the Tuesday Market Place a street leads to St

Nicholas Chapel, which is a chapel-of-ease to St Margaret's Church. It is Perpendicular and was built on to an earlier tower in 1419. Inside, the air of space is impressive. The slender arcades scarcely obstruct the vista and there is no chancel arch. The Chapel is a complete contrast to another elsewhere in the town: the Red Mount Chapel, which stands amid the trees of the Walks—avenues laid out on the site of the old defences of the town—boulevards, as a native of Lynn once described them to me. The Red Mount Chapel is a tiny building only 17 feet long, with a fan-vaulted roof, built inside a slightly larger brick building, with stairs between the two. It dates from 1485 and is a perfect church in miniature. It was intended for the use of pilgrims.

King Street, which leads back to the town from the Tuesday Market Place, is lined with seventeenth- and eighteenth-century buildings, but its chief glory is the Guildhall of St George in which Shakespeare is believed to have acted. After being a warehouse for stage scenery for years, it was restored for use as a theatre, concert hall and art gallery and is the centre for the King's Lynn Festival.

There is more evidence of Henry Bell's work at Clifton House, a little farther on in Queen's Street. Flat on the narrow street, it has a doorway ornamented with two columns twisted like barley sugar. The house dates from various periods, and at the back is a five-storey watch-tower which looks over the river. It was once a merchant's house, but the present name only dates from 1883 when it was given to it by the owner because the previous owner was a William Clifton. On the same side of the road is Thoresby College, originally founded in 1500 for priests, but mostly dating from the seventeenth century.

There are a number of good shops in Lynn and the fact that several of them display the Royal Warrant is a reminder that members of the Royal Family have for generations patronized them. The Queen Mother in particular has also taken interest in the King's Lynn Festival and in the local Grammar School.

That King's Lynn was the only town in Norfolk to be besieged during the Civil War is no surprise in view of its strategic position. It is the gateway to Norfolk from the north and west as well as from the sea. It has thus something of the nature of a frontier town.

There could scarcely be a greater change in the country to the west and east of Lynn. To the east is the rolling countryside of Norfolk; well wooded and cultivated, with large country houses and estates: a pleasant place in which to live. The Marshland and the Fens to the west are sharply different from the rest of Norfolk. It is surprising that boundary changes have not recognized the fact and handed the whole area to the Isle of Ely, which is so similar in physical features, methods of farming, way of life and much else. For a long time it has been part of the Diocese of Ely and it is towards Ely, Wisbech and King's Lynn that the inhabitants turn for their needs. When I talked to a native of Terrington St Clement, I was told that the people in the eastern part of that village look towards Lynn for their shopping and entertainment and those in the western part of the village look towards Wisbech.

That part of Norfolk which is known as the Marshland lies to the west of the River Great Ouse and extends to Wisbech, in Cambridgeshire. It is here that the country is truly flat, a district of rich silt, with the peat of the true fen country to the south. To the north, across mud flats and salt marshes from which the sea is retreating, is the Wash. There is a strong case for the Wash to be reclaimed in the same way that the Dutch have reclaimed the Zuyder Zee, but governments have been too timid to start. Owing to the tendency of the eastern side of England to sink, experts have forecast that if nothing is done in the meanwhile it may become too expensive to drain the rich fen country by the end of this century. The land is already below sea level and is shrinking rapidly through the drainage of the peat soil and the wastage due to the loss of earth which is removed with the root crops. The plan for the Wash envisages a large fresh-water lake which would provide eastern England with much-needed water, and there would be thousands of acres of land available for farming to help make up for that being lost through urbanization. Norfolk would have better communication with the North, and a number of other advantages would follow.

A journey from Wisbech to King's Lynn or Downham Market reveals the rich soil and the good use to which it is put. Fruit orchards abound, and crops are often taken from the land between the trees. There are market gardens and a big flower industry, run in many cases by Dutchmen or people of Dutch extraction. I have not regarded it as attractive scenery, but when once I took some Australian friends there they displayed unexpected delight and interest in the comparison of the fruit-growing methods with their own. It is a country of dykes instead of hedges and walls, of prosperous-looking houses standing alone, surrounded by their fields or glass houses. The small villages straggle along the roads or along the banks of water courses. A neglected canal divides Norfolk from Cambridgeshire as the southern boundary of this area. To the west, the River Nene forms the boundary with Lincolnshire, which here closely resembles the Marshland. To the north one can see nothing because the horizon is so low and the sea is so far from the main King's Lynn to Sutton Bridge road, from which *culs-de-sac* lead to remote hamlets.

The great glory of the Marshland is in its churches. Norfolk has hundreds of fine ancient churches, but surely none finer than these. The roll call of the names of the parishes has an air about it. Terrington St Clement has already been mentioned, and there is Terrington St John. Other names seem to go in pairs; Tilney All Saints and Tilney St Lawrence; Walpole St Peter and Walpole St Andrew; Walsoken and West Walton; and the quartet, Wiggenhall St Germans, Wiggenhall St Mary Magdalen, Wiggenhall St Mary the Virgin and Wiggenhall St Peter. These are not just the names of the churches, but the names of the villages as well. One of the best descriptions of a village of this group can be found in that excellent detective story by Dorothy L. Sayers, *The Nine Tailors*. Not content with the wealth of names, she has invented another of the sonorous style, Fenchurch St Paul, and has even had a picture of the fictitious church drawn so convincingly that it would take its place quite naturally among its neighbours. It shares features with Walpole St Peter and Terrington St Clement, but the angel roof must surely have received some inspiration from that of St Wendreda's, March, over the Cambridgeshire border.

All these parishes and more are in an irregular triangle about 14 miles from north to south and about seven miles from east to west, amounting to 54,000 acres. Notice the prefix Wal- which occurs in several of the names. It derives from an earthen 'wall' or bank, known as the Roman Bank, which was raised to protect the Marshland from inundation by the sea. Though doubt has been expressed as

to whether the Roman Bank was the work of Romans, it must certainly have been there before the Norman Conquest for the parishes
existed then and Walsoken Church dates from the late Norman
period and West Walton was built about 1240.

Much of the traffic from the Midlands to Norfolk passes through
Wisbech, and the major part of it travels along the road from Wisbech to King's Lynn. A detour of a mile or so to either side provides a
lesson in church architecture and an uplifting experience aesthetic-
ally. Walsoken is virtually a suburb of Wisbech and Pevsner describes
its church as the grandest Norman parish church of Norfolk—
presumably excluding Wymondham, which was originally a monastery. The late Norman arcade and chancel arch are impressive. On
the other side of the main road to the north is West Walton, a perfect example of the Early English style, built of stone (it must be
remembered that there is not even flint in the Marshland and building stone had to be imported from Northamptonshire), with a massive detached tower—a necessary precaution where the foundation
might be precarious. There is plenty of dog-tooth moulding and
stiff-leaf foliage carving to attest the early thirteenth-century date.
Most of the other interesting churches lie on the same side of the
main road. The finest of them all is Walpole St Peter; it is particularly impressive outside, with its 14 clerestory windows on each
side. Its massive tower, which is earlier than the main building, belongs to the Decorated period, while the rest is Perpendicular. It
stands in a beautifully kept churchyard; a feature which catches the
eye is the wide passage beneath the chancel, where the rings used
for tethering horses during service can still be seen. In the room over
the very fine south porch, there are the benches of a little school-
room where the village children were taught until 1812, when a
proper school was built for them. Inside the church, the fittings are a
precious heritage. One enters a space screened from the nave by a
seventeenth-century wooden screen with doors, and in this ante-
chapel there is a fine Tudor font with a Jacobean cover with doors
which open in its sides. The old seating in the nave is complete, and
in the side aisles the benches rise in tiers facing inwards. There are
some misericords in the chancel and some lovely brass chandeliers.
The eye is drawn towards the east end, where a flight of some dozen

steps rises to the altar. Was this raised position of the altar the cause or effect of the passage beneath it? In one corner of the church stands an unusual relic, a kind of sentry box which was used by the parson on wet days when taking funeral services at the grave-side. After a period when this magnificent building suffered from lack of sufficient funds to keep it in repair, it has recently enjoyed a revival and now looks well cared for. It is worth travelling many miles to see.

Over the Roman Bank, the church at Terrington St Clement is a rival to that of Walpole St Peter. It belongs to the Perpendicular period, but incorporates parts built two centuries before. Like West Walton, the tower is detached from the main building, though in this case the gap is very small, whereas at West Walton there is a considerable distance between the tower and the church. The church at Tilney All Saints dates back to the twelfth century and has many features of interest. It has recently been restored. All the Marshland churches are worth visiting; it would take up too much space to describe them all. Walpole St Andrew has a curious little living chamber on the roof which must have housed the priest; Wiggenhall St Germans has some fine early sixteenth-century benches, and so has Wiggenhall St Mary the Virgin. On the southern edge of Marshland, both Upwell and Outwell churches are built of Barnack stone and have good roofs. Outwell has some fifteenth-century glass. They lie on the road from Wisbech to Downham Market—a good alternative route to Central Norfolk which avoids the heaviest traffic.

The whole of Marshland and the parishes east of the River Ouse as far as Stoke Ferry are in the Diocese of Ely—which shows that the ecclesiastical authorities were more realistic than their civil counterparts, who included them in the county of Norfolk, administered from Norwich 50 miles away.

Of the inhabitants of the Fens, one might say that the problem of taming water is always present in their minds, whereas the lack of it concerns the rest of Norfolk. A few years ago, a huge new channel was dug west of Downham Market to help the water to flow away, and nearby, another channel, dug some 20 years ago, brings water from Barton Mills in Suffolk along the contour line through Lakenheath, catching water from the higher ground of the forest area and relieving the already over-burdened rivers. Lord Peter Wimsey, who solved the mystery in *The Nine Tailors*, and who was the hero of Dorothy Sayers' other books, was brother to the fictitious Duke of Denver, but Denver is better known for its sluice which releases or holds back the waters of the Great Ouse according to the state of the tides. Upon it depends the safety of thousands of square miles of Fens, some of the richest and most important farm land in England. It was not always like this, for not until the seventeenth century were the fens drained, and cultivation took the place of the old pursuits of wild-fowling and fishing which bred a race of men somewhat like those who more recently inhabited the Norfolk Broads. Tales of their hard way of living are still told by their successors who worked on the land before modern scientific methods of mechanical farming became fashionable. The men who could dig the dykes beautifully by hand were known as 'slodgers', an example of an onomatopoeic word which conveys the sound of a spadeful of clay being slapped on a bank. Within present memory living conditions in the Fens were bad, but the introduction of electricity and better transport have improved matters radically.

The eastern boundary between the Marshland and the Fens on the one side and the higher land of Norfolk on the other is the A.10 road from Ely to King's Lynn. It enters the county at Brandon Creek, where the Little Ouse flows into the Great Ouse, and after crossing two or three miles of typical fenland, with the level of the shrunken peat soil well below that of the road, it climbs to the higher ground at Southery and continues at a height of from 30 to 50 feet above sea level, while the fen to the west is at, or below, sea level. Except for the villages of Runcton Holme and Watlington, which are rather like outposts, there is little building between the road and the Great Ouse. The road winds through trees in many places and is pretty, particularly at Ryston and Stow Bardolph. The churches of Fordham, Denver, Downham Market, Wimbotsham and Stow Bardolph are all built of carstone, which is believed to have been quarried at Bexwell to the east of Downham Market. Bexwell Church has a round tower of the same material.

In Ryston Park, close to Denver, stands Kett's Oak, which was associated with Kett's Rebellion in 1549. It is in better shape than the tree of the same name between Wymondham and Norwich, which is on its last legs although only a descendant of the original. Denver is, as we have seen, the site of Denver Sluice, which controls the outlet for the water of the Great Ouse and the New Bedford River which, between them, drain hundreds of square miles in Norfolk, Suffolk, Cambridgeshire, Huntingdon and Bedfordshire.

Downham Market is a small market town with few really ancient buildings. The cast-iron Victorian clock tower in the centre of the town, erected in 1878, is old enough to have acquired the status of a period piece and the eighteenth-century front of the Castle Hotel stands strategically placed to face the traveller who drove up the main street, which until recently was part of the A.10.

A few miles east of Downham Market on the road to Swaffham is the village of Fincham, with its Perpendicular church. The porch is dated 1503 and, with the south side facing the road, is decorated with battlements and flushwork, while inside the tall arcades support a hammerbeam roof. Perhaps the most interesting feature of the building is the square Norman font decorated by representations of the Nativity, the Magi, Baptism, and Adam and Eve on the four sides. Each subject is shown in an arcade of three arches. There is a strong resemblance to the font at Burnham Deepdale on the North Norfolk coast.

Returning to the A.10, Stow Bardolph has a church which is worth a visit, mainly for its monuments. It lies near Stowe Hall, the home of the Hare family for over 400 years; they have left their mark on both the church and the village. The Hare Chapel was built in 1624 on the north side of the church; the most beautiful of the carefully preserved monuments it contains is the one to Sir Ralph Hare, who was knighted at the coronation of King James I. A curiosity in the Chapel is a life-size wax effigy of Sarah Hare who died in 1744 as a result, it was alleged, of pricking her finger while doing needlework on the Sabbath Day. The effigy, dressed in the costume of the period, was made at her direction and is kept in a glass case.

While the churches of the villages in this area nearly all contain Norman features, North Runcton, nearer to King's Lynn, is one of the very few eighteenth-century churches in the county. It was

26 *Oxborough Hall: late fifteenth-century gatehouse*
27 *King's Lynn: the western towers of St Margaret's Church*
28 *King's Lynn: the Custom's House*

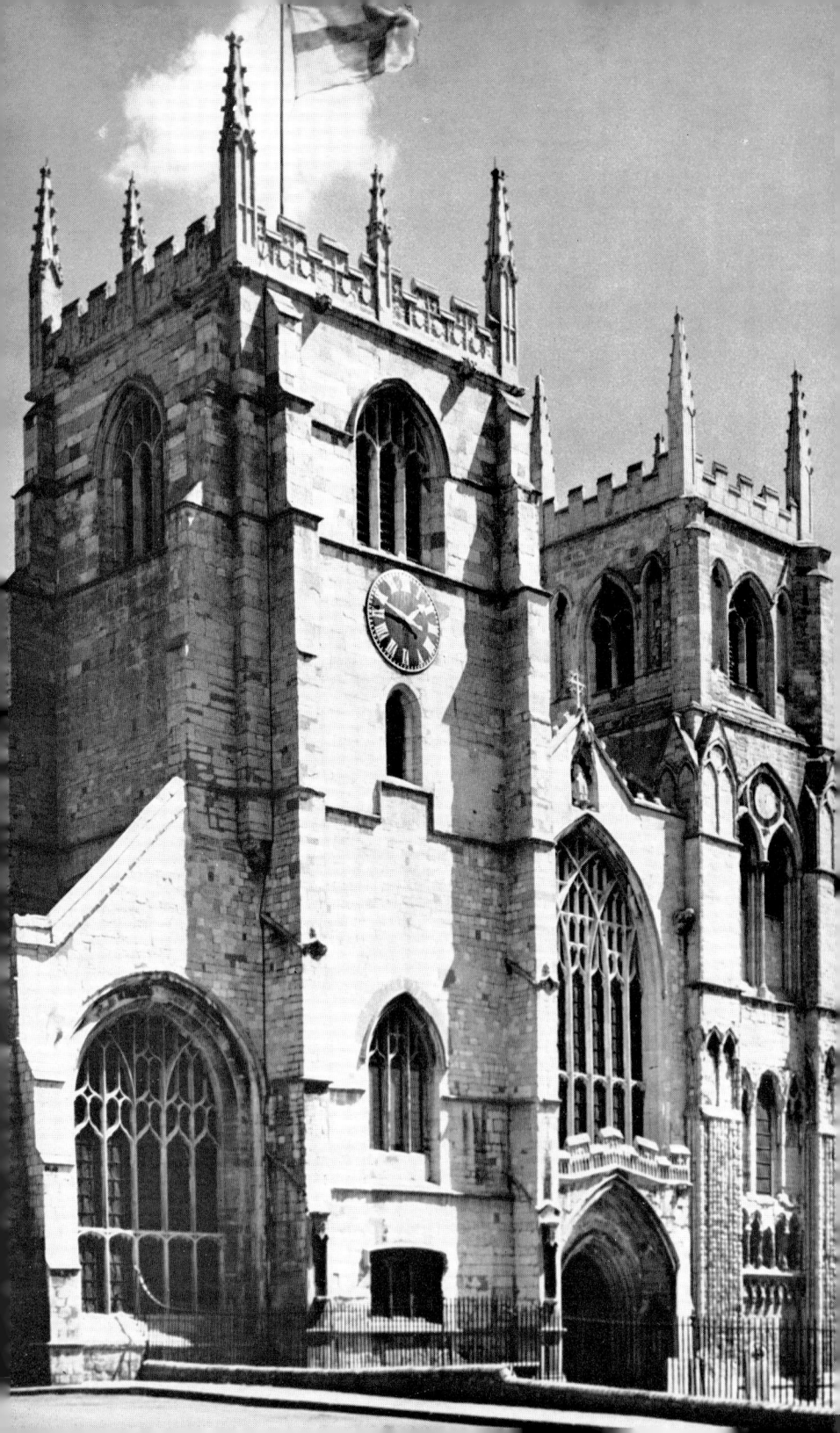

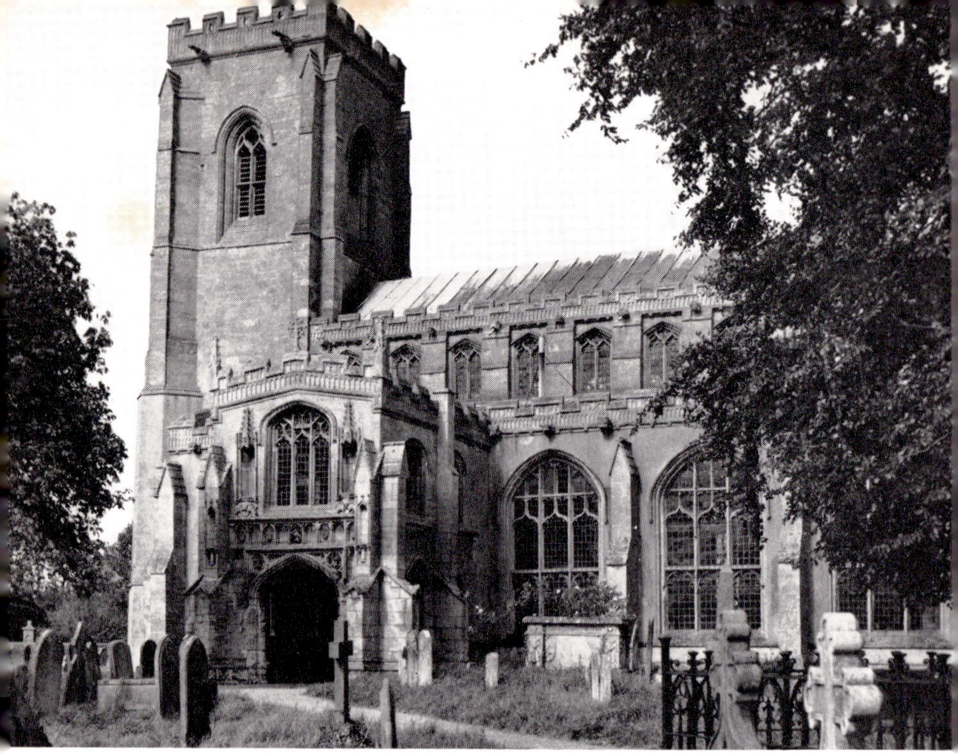

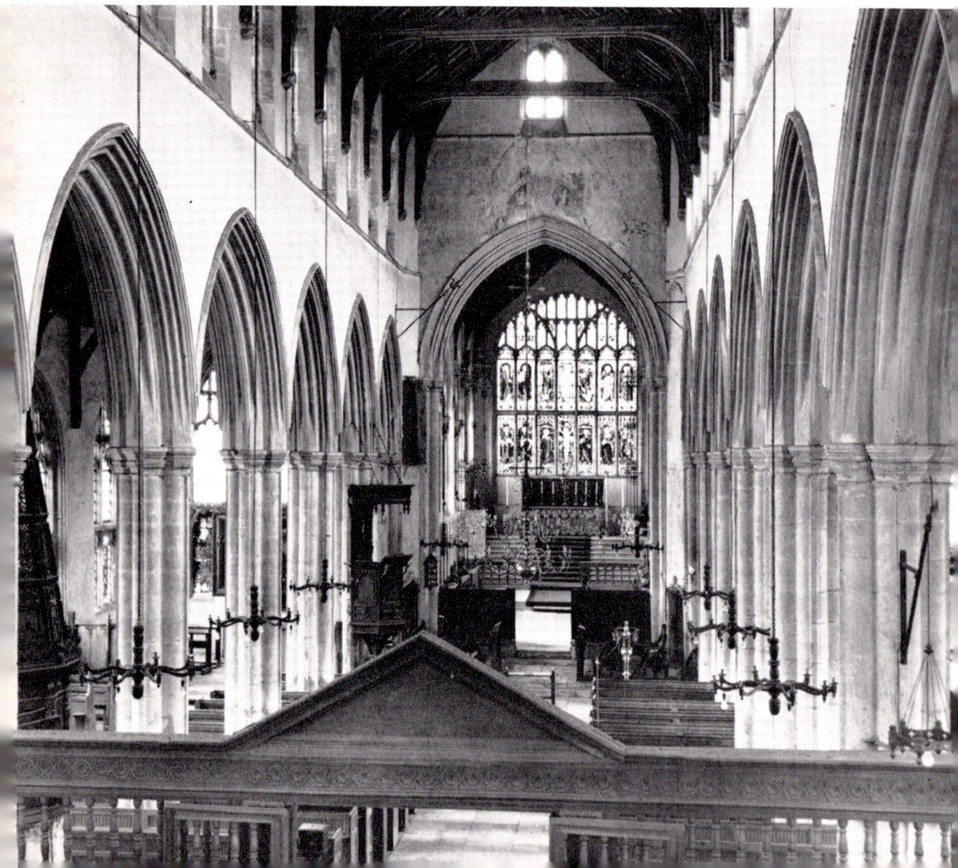

built between 1703 and 1713, probably by the King's Lynn architect, Henry Bell. The design and the classical interior were influenced by Wren's churches. Runcton Hall, nearby, was largely built by the architect Anthony Salvin in 1835 for Daniel Gurney, a younger brother of Elizabeth Fry of Earlham, Norwich. The house is still inhabited by members of the family. A delightful and amusing account of life there in the mid-Victorian period can be found in a book entitled *Life Among the Troubridges*, by Laura Troubridge, a granddaughter of Daniel Gurney.

Close to North Runcton, on the King's Lynn to Swaffham road, is the village of Middleton. A picturesque house, Middleton Towers, which incorporates a fourteenth-century gatehouse, stands to the north of the village. The next village on this road, some two miles to the east, is East Winch. Osbert Lancaster, who is patron of the living of East Winch and Lord of the Manor, has described the place as it was in his childhood in his autobiography *All Done from Memory*. As at Fincham, we have strayed away from the corridor of Greensand which makes the country bordering the A.10 different in appearance to the rest of Norfolk. It is very pleasant country, sandwiched between the flat, inhospitable Fens on one side and the open more barren soil of Breckland on the other: a land which attracted settlement in early times when both the Fens and the Breckland were forbidding. The Breckland and the forests of central Norfolk provided an effective barrier for centuries and the psychological effect of this has remained.

Some three miles south of East Winch along a minor road leading to Marham is the gatehouse of Pentney Priory, an imposing building in good repair. The Priory, founded in the early twelfth century, has disappeared. If we return to the main King's Lynn to Swaffham road through Pentney village there is a turning to the North signposted to Sandringham which takes us through a number of pleasant villages: East Walton, Gayton, Grimston and Hillington. To the right is the heathland of the higher chalk country, sparsely populated, with large stony fields and copses of trees. The route we are following is part of the Icknield Way and the Peddars Way runs parallel with it about four miles to the east. At Hillington our way is barred by the grounds of Hillington Hall, which has been demolished,

29   *Walpole St Peter: tower and south porch*
30   *Walpole St Peter: interior of nave*

but the imposing entrance gate is supposed to have been one of the town gates of King's Lynn removed here many years ago.

At either Gayton, Grimston or Hillington we could return to King's Lynn through pleasant country, the roads from both Hillington and Grimston cross Roydon Common, which is one of the most open stretches of country in Norfolk. A turning just south of Grimston leads through a hamlet named Pottrow where numerous examples of a partially glazed ware dating from the thirteenth and fourteenth centuries have been found. The glaze is green and nearly 20 almost perfect examples of gallon jars, some quite undamaged, have been found in a well.

King's Lynn, the natural exit from Norfolk, seems a suitable place to bid 'fare thee well' as the Norfolkman would say. It is not 'goodbye' for the visitor to Norfolk comes again, either to revisit the spots he has learned to love, or to explore the rich treasure which can occupy years, be it the study of its ancient buildings, its natural history, or the many other things which provide such a diversity of interest. The resident may safely be assumed to return once he has taken root. Norfolk is typical England, but it prides itself in being different' in some subtle way. Long may it continue to be so.

INDEX

The numerals in **bold** refer to illustration numbers

Index

Index

Index